WIDOWHOOD
AND OTHER ALTERED STATES

WIDOWHOOD AND OTHER ALTERED STATES

Coming of Age at Seventy-Plus

Jacqueline Sideman Guttman

llustrations by Christine Finley

Full Court Press
Englewood Cliffs, New Jersey

First Edition

Published in the United States of America
by Full Court Press, 601 Palisade Avenue,
Englewood Cliffs, NJ 07632
fullcourtpress.com

ISBN 979-8-218-47250-4
Library of Congress Control No. 2024921692

Editing and book design by Barry Sheinkopf

"My Coffee with Amir" was originally published in excerpted form in *Autumn Years*, September 2020.

This book is dedicated

to my bereavement group gang—Sheila, Gloria, Donna, and Barbara—and to all the women and men who put themselves back together and soldier on after going from We to Me.

And for Howard.

Acknowledgements

I want to thank Peter Bricklebank, and the Pure Critique writing workshop at the Hudson Valley Writers Center, for guidance and encouragement; Chris Finley for her wonderful drawings; My bereavement group at Jewish Family and Children's Services of Northern New Jersey for loving my "stories"; Julie Baraz for her enthusiastic support at the start; Barbara Conover, without whom I would not have made any progress in the beginning; Jennie Katsaros, friend and retired editor, for her support and encouragement; and Barry Sheinkopf, for actually making it happen. Also, I am so fortunate to have a loving and supportive family, especially my grandson Franklin, who shares my love of writing, and is so excited that his grandmother is producing a book!

Table of Contents

From We to Me

ALTHOUGH THERE IS NO DENYING the tragedy of the death of a spouse at a young age, less attention is given to the so-called norm: losing one's spouse—usually a husband—at a point in life when it's far more difficult to reinvent oneself, after decades of marriage.

In particular, life for an older widow usually lacks the stabilizing structure of a job or the necessity of caring for children. Women who married in the 1960s and even the full-of-change '70s, many of whom had lived for decades within a traditional structure in which the "guy stuff" included everything from paying bills to killing bugs, now must learn to become totally self-reliant. And we do it, most of us, pleased that we are so competent and furious that we have no choice, while often also dealing with broken hearts both figuratively and literally, diabetes, joint replacements, high blood pressure, and, sometimes, the financial issues that often accompany these and other problems.

After the initial period of getting through the funeral and its aftermath, many widows and widowers alike are overwhelmed by the realization that they have become a "me," after decades of life as a "we." Whether a spouse or lover died quickly or gradually, the new state of singlehood comes as a shock. I attended a bereavement support group. Each of us arrived looking dazed—that deer-in-headlights look. I found it fascinating and wonderful to watch members return to being themselves—not to "recover," for the loss never leaves us, but to gradually find the pieces of who we were and slowly put them back together. The best thing we did there was laugh together, with no one to judge whether it was "too early" or "inappropriate," and four of the women and I became fast friends. We still meet almost every Sunday for dinner and sometimes an excursion, and even take vacations together. We have each other's back, and sometimes I'm more comfortable asking them for help then I am with much longer-term friends. We went through a crucible together, and it welded us.

Women in the group related that they often found themselves good for lunches with other women, but that dinner dates with couple-friends tended to taper off quickly. Men, conversely, described being badgered by well-meaning friends who were ready to introduce them to a "replacement" while they were still mourning. The particulars may differ, but the feelings of loss and dislocation are not exclusive to either gender. I do admit, however, to having been struck dumb when a grieving widower commented sadly that he guessed a time would come when he'd *have* to find someone else, as though it were a chore, which perhaps it is. A dear male friend of mine, short, bald, beachball stomach, and OK, brilliant, who found an absolutely lovely woman a year and a half after the death of his wife, told me that, no matter how this new woman makes him happy, it will always be making the best of a bad situation. But "have to find someone?" What woman could or would make such a statement? Whether we are passive or aggressive, most of us have to wait to be found. And given the ratio of men to women at an older stage, most of us, statistically in fact, are not found; we remain single for the rest of our lives.

As an observer of spousal loss as well as a participant, I note that many of us—whether women or men—tended to put our spouses on pedestals. I have heard (and have made) comments like, "He was a great scholar," "She was beautiful," "I wish I could tell him all he meant to me," and "She always made me happy." As an exercise, I sometimes remind myself of my husband's foibles, like his screaming and swearing at the television set during the baseball, football, hockey, and basketball seasons, which overlap, meaning I never got a rest, or his ineptness when trying to assemble a piece of furniture; it keeps me sane and makes me laugh. I strongly recommend it.

My real survival tool has been writing about the varied

experiences of a newly single life, of coming of age at 70-plus. Some of these essays deal with living alone, handling health or disability issues, taking care of home repairs, and searching for male companionship; others are general observations on life, but with a glance at loss and survival.

The essay that follows, "Cemetery Shopping," was begun two days prior to my husband's death, at the suggestion of my son. I finished it a few days later, amid tears and a bit of laughter. Another, "A Case of the Bends," focuses humorously on coping with physical limitations without the aid of a helpmate. A third, "Car Virgin No More," expresses pride at shopping successfully for a first car on my own. And of course, an exploration of widowhood must at least speculate on the possibility of finding a new special someone, as in "Hope Springs Eternal."

Each of us goes along in a unique way and gradually reinvents ourself, developing a different but satisfying life. Yet every now and then a painful reminder jumps up and smacks us in the face. It's finding an old can of baked beans in your pantry when you hate beans, or coming upon a lacy bra that he loved. Do I keep it? Do I wear it? On a date? It's detouring in order to avoid driving past the hospital where she died, or dreading the walk down your front path because that's where he fell. Or awakening to see the empty other side of the bed, or seeing older couples shopping together in the mall, often holding hands. Whether it's from love or because one has balance issues or both, it's still a reminder of what we no longer have.

Death has many euphemisms. I had always thought of them as a scourge, but my stance has softened as I've reflected on my husband's death. For me, it's not that he passed, or passed away, or lost his battle, or any of the other substitute expressions that deny the reality. Stubbornly I say, "Howard died on January 10, 2017." My parents used the word "gone" when someone died. When I was young, I thought it was silly, but there is no gone like the gone of death—I learned that first when they died, and now again, with the death of my husband. The one euphemism I have accepted and even use is "lost." I lost my husband on January 10, 2017. "Lost" works for me because, even now, I have the feeling that, if only I knew where to look, maybe I'd find him. I think of something Joan Didion wrote in *The Year of Magical Thinking*; she kept her husband's shoes for a year, until she realized that she kept them so that they'd be there when he returned and needed them. When I first read the book, while my husband was still living, I found it unbearably depressing, even annoying; now it makes sense. That's how we change—with the changes in our lives.

Given the realities of widowhood, we might as well laugh, and share our downs and ups, our defeats and triumphs. Note that I mention triumphs last; that's no accident. We will triumph because we must. Anything else is unacceptable.

Cemetery Shopping

TWO DAYS BEFORE HOWARD DIED, my sons Edward and Marc and I checked out a couple of cemeteries. It was a macabre thing to do, perhaps, but necessary, for I was having second thoughts about where to bury him, and my sons wanted me to be comfortable with the decision.

We left the hospital and drove to Riverside Cemetery, off I-80 in Lodi, New Jersey, where Howard had always assumed we both would be buried. Though Riverside actually is by the side of a small river, it was not exactly my idea of a bucolic permanent resting place. There had been no I-80 in the mid-twentieth century when Jacob Guttman, Howard's grandfather, purchased a grand plot with room for 20-plus graves. Now, however, the traffic goes roaring by around the clock on a highway that extends 3,000 miles from New Jersey to California, and the road immediately outside the cemetery is filled with gas stations, diners, day-rate motels, and strip malls.

It had just snowed and was a frigid fifteen degrees outside. In fact, prior to our cemetery jaunt, I'd been sitting in my husband's hospice room, contemplating how to look appropriate for a funeral without freezing—maybe leggings under my long black skirt and fleece-lined boots, along with the sheared muskrat coat I had not worn in a few years for fear of getting stoned by PETA folks. My friend Marsha had even gone hat shopping for me.

I'd looked at a map of Riverside and my eye had fallen on Naomi Walk. It felt familiar though I had not been there in at least ten years. We drove into the cemetery and up the road that my senses told me was correct. No Naomi, but we did find Ruth. "Aha!" I said, "here is Ruth; Naomi must be nearby." My sons looked at me quizzically until Marc remembered that the biblical Naomi had told her mother-in-law Ruth, "Whither thou goest, there shall I go." Searching for our plot, we drove aimlessly around the empty (of living human habitation) white cemetery, hearing nothing but the crunch of tires on snow.

Marc pulled up the map on his iPhone, and there it was, back near Ruth as I'd thought. We took a likely road and, sure enough, found Naomi Walk. But "Walk" meant just that; we could not easily drive to the site from where we were. Enveloped in their parkas, hoods over their heads, Marc and Ed each walked the Walk in opposite directions. Marc waved, at a spot just where I though it should be.

Then he dove back into the warm car while Ed took a look, brushing off the snow on one of the footstones—his grandmother's, as it turned out. When he came back, we drove to a closer spot, and all three of us got out. Huddling at the site, we saw that the big family headstone was leaning forward, thanks to a tree that had apparently grown beyond expectations. We were not certain who else was there other than my in-laws—except Jacob and Sally, Howard's grandparents. Although they had lived apart, they were side by side in death.

We parked at the Charles Addams-like house that serves as the administrative office. A hand-written sign mysteriously directed us to enter through the back door, where we clambered over cartons of cemetery brochures and emerged into a nice, warm, carpeted office area. There we were shown the computerized plot and its occupants, who also included Aunt Lillian and Uncle Irving (who, it is said, also had little use for each other), Uncle Joe—though none of his three wives—and other assorted relatives. There was no one from our generation despite the fact that some, including Howard, were named on the computer as "customers." Some had already died and were interred elsewhere; others, I was quite sure, had no intention of reposing at Riverside.

Perhaps my most important concern was that, while I was keeping a vigil over Howard along with his beloved cousin Krystyna, she had told me stories of his childhood and not-so-loving treatment by his parents and uncles. I saw no reason to have Howard lying in perpetuity with people who had mistreated him. And I definitely did not want to be there with them.

Meanwhile, hedging my bets, I'd emailed my friend Sam, keeper of the plot owned by our synagogue. He'd told me that although the plot was sold out, he'd kept a few graves available "for emergencies." I wasn't sure what constituted an emergency in a graveyard, but apparently we qualified. I told him I'd get back to him.

Our next stop: Cedar Park in Paramus. Unlike the venerable Riverside, where every road and path bears a biblical name, my synagogue's site was located on the far less imaginative "Block 38." I admit that this made it a lot easier to find. It was also easy because, sadly, we had been to several burials there in the last few years. We were greeted silently by our friends Fred, Barbara, and David, all of whom have headstones with a blank side for their spouses to use in the future. You might think this plan a bit creepy, but we agreed that we preferred the more open feeling. And Marc said he thought it would be nice to have Dad buried amid our coffee-klatch. We decided to overrule Howard's assumption that we would be with his family.

The decision made, I hurriedly said, "I'd better call Sam right away!"

Ed said, "I just had the same thought!" What—would he sell it to someone else if we didn't grab it while we had the chance? The three of us looked at each other and, sitting in the car by the piece of land under which we would soon be burying our much-loved husband and father, started laughing hysterically. We laughed and laughed. It felt wonderful. We all agreed that Howard would have loved the whole ridiculous business. I emailed Sam that we wanted to bury Howard at Cedar Park.

We returned to the hospital. As Ed had stayed over the previous night, I sent him home. Going to Howard's room, Marc and I joined cousin Krys and my sister as well as the hospice's generously sized bereavement counselor, Rabbi Steven ("Call me Steve") Kapnik, who had been talking to them and praying over Howard for an hour. After crushing me in a bear hug, he sat with me for another hour, talking about the legacy my husband and I had created—on and on, *ad exhaustion*—but his kindness and advice also made it possible for us to leave Howard and go home to sleep, rather than continuing our overnight vigil.

The following evening, Krys, Edward, and I sat with unconscious Howard; Marc had gone home to rest. We waited until 10:30, wanting but not wanting to leave. I kissed Howard's eyes, nose, cheeks, and forehead. I stroked his hair. Weeping a bit, I told him I loved him and would miss him always, but that I would be alright, that the boys would take good care of me. (I had no idea what I was talking about.) Then Ed kissed him and spoke to him. Then Krys. Pulled back by a need to be the last person to kiss him, I returned to the bed and kissed his forehead once again, pressing my face to his. At the nurse's suggestion we turned off the light, something we had not done prior to that night.

I got the call at 4:00 a.m. Howard, always a bit obsessed with the weather and ever considerate of my comfort, had waited for the temperature to rise. The following afternoon we stood in the cemetery on a balmy 58-degree January day.

The fur coat stayed in the closet. I didn't need the hat.

A Thousand Napkins

IT'S ASTONISHING HOW LONG things last when you live alone. Two weeks for a roll of toilet paper. Nearly that long before you must take out the garbage—another interesting but sad fact of living alone for the first time. And then there are the napkins, the endless napkins.

When we returned from the cemetery after my husband's funeral, awaiting us were platters of sandwiches and cold-cuts that had been ordered by my sister, as I, according to my rabbi, was not to be responsible for anything. Turkey, roast beef, pastrami, potato salad, cole slaw, beverages—I've forgotten what else, as I was not involved in the selection. A helpful friend had received the food delivery for us, so that all would be ready when we wearily arrived home. Another friend, who is lovely, efficient, and cost conscious in equal parts, had picked up plastic ware and paper napkins at Costco, where everything is sold in bulk. She wanted to be sure we would not run out of anything. It was a *big* package of napkins, and they lasted throughout the *Shiva*, or Jewish mourning period. Each day and evening, as people stopped by or came to the brief religious service, we provided the customary refreshments, from deli sandwiches to cookies and coffee.

When *Shiva* ended, the remaining food was frozen or distributed to family and all the plastic goods put away. The only thing remaining was the napkins. It gave me a pang when I began using them as my regular napkins, but tossing them would have been both foolish and disrespectful to the environment. So I'd refill my napkin holder every couple of weeks, each time wishing the napkins would get used up, as they were a daily reminder of my loss.

The problem was that, not only did they never seem to diminish, but that, also, I hated them. They were not the everyday square household variety. Pre-folded into rectangles that resembled dinner napkins, they had pretensions of grandeur—until they were opened. Not that I have a napkin fetish, but they were single-ply, and the ply was thin. They protected clothing from little other than crumbs. Look at them sideways, or just unfold them to place in your lap, and a hole would appear. Spill something, or just wipe peanut butter off your finger, and it went right through. Utterly useless and a constant irritant.

Months went by. Howard's clothing was donated, his office cleaned out, but the napkins remained. I rejoiced when I realized that the topmost layer was gone, and I eagerly pulled back the paper to begin making forays into the second half of the package.

In October, nine months after the funeral, we had the unveiling of Howard's headstone. Although I had intended this to be observed by family and a few close friends, twenty-seven people joined us at the cemetery. Again, we returned to the house and the deli platters. Ordered by me this time, they now included some Middle-Eastern-flavored side dishes. And still, there were my faithful napkins, stacked neatly, folds in place, waiting to ill-perform their designated task.

In December, on Hanukah, the napkins stayed in the package as, with relief and a sense of vengeance, I brought out my blue and white dreidel-decorated cloth napkins to add to my holiday-themed paper plates. What a pleasure! We could drop food into our laps with impunity, unconcerned about the possibility of stains leaking onto our clothes.

January rolled around. On the one-year anniversary of my husband's death, I gazed, disbelieving, at the still substantial stack of unsubstantial napkins. I did the math. Since I don't eat every meal at home, let's say I have 15 meals per week at which I use a napkin: 15 times 50—figuring I'm away here and there—makes 750. Would these cursed napkins never disappear? I even discussed them with my kids and their wives, telling them I could not wait to get back to my usual Bounty napkins. Scornfully, they told me that Bounty was ridiculous, and that Vanity Fair was the answer. Did I know that they harbored such strong opinions about napkin brands? Now that I think of it, Howard would have hated them, having grown up in very elegant surroundings on Central Park West. In his home, such napkins would have been unceremoniously dumped. In my home, we were of necessity more frugal.

I tried to use the napkins indiscriminately, taking two when one would do, blowing my nose in them (they are soft and absorbent), and wiping the counter with them. But, at thirteen months, they are still here. To make matters worse, when I took out the most recent batch, I checked the number of napkins in the package. To my horror, I discovered that it's a pack not of 1,000, but of 1,250! Let's see: if I have, say, 400 left, and I use 20 per week, I still would have another 20 weeks of napkin-wrestling.

So check back with me this coming July, which will be a year and a half after my husband's death. If I'm gnashing my teeth and have stains on my clothing, you'll know I was my usual inaccurate mathematical self and figured it wrong. If I'm smiling and spotless, however, the message will be clear. My well-meaning but useless napkins will have finally gone, to be replaced by the highest quality, most elegant paper serviettes I can find: Vanity Fair.

THE NAPKINS WERE USED UP IN AUGUST, 2018, just a month after my projected date. Though I hated them, I'll never forget them, for their memory is intertwined with memories of Howard. And just as I could get really annoyed with him, the napkins provided an object for my grieving. Dare I say I miss them? Definitely not.

A Case of the Bends

WHY, WHEN I TAKE OFF A SWEATER and put it on a chair, does it immediately slide onto the floor? I've been thinking a lot about that lately, more so since I've begun living alone. Not that Howard, my late husband, ever picked things up, for he had his own problems with bending. I would sometimes leave a fallen item on the floor for days just to see if he'd retrieve it, but eventually I'd give in and pick it up.

To the young and able-bodied, bending does not sound like much of an undertaking; you just lean over and retrieve the object—no big deal. To many of us older folk, though, it's a small project. My husband's bending difficulties and impaired balance necessitated his using a walker. I, on the other hand, could do the bend, but my arthritic fingers could not, for example, grab a penny from the floor. I could do it if I really needed to, but as I've said, it was actually a project. I might, for example, lick my thumb so that the coin would stick to it just long enough for me to grab it between thumb and index finger. Small items could remain on the floor for two weeks, until the cleaning man came.

But I digress. Back to my sweater. I bend over, pick up the sweater, and put it back on the chair. As I watch, I see a sleeve begin to creep over the edge, gathering momentum as the rest of the garment follows. I quickly grab it and either put it away or try again, carefully making sure there are no pieces hanging off the chair edge. Sometimes I even command it, "Stay!" and it usually listens to me.

I've consulted with my contemporaries, and they've noticed a similar phenomenon—things definitely conspire to fall on the floor. I analyze it: Are fabrics more slippery than they used to be? Are synthetics more slippery than silk, wool, or cotton? Aha! Perhaps there is some finishing product that adds a sheen or otherwise enhances clothing these days.

The problem, however, does not end with clothing.

Another scenario: I come home and put my purse on the hall table. I open it to take out my cell phone that I can't be without, foolishly leaving the zipper open. The moment I turn my back, an evil gremlin tips over the purse, causing it to fall on the floor and disgorge all its contents. A major bending operation is necessary if I'm to retrieve my wallet, reading glasses, pen, receipts, business cards, appointment cards, keys, assorted coins. The coins, of course, include the truly challenging dimes. Who can pick up a dime? Actually, who cares about dimes? When was the last time anything cost ten cents?

And there's the wastepaper basket. Don't we all toss things into the basket from across the room, feeling a small measure of satisfaction when the object swishes in? My husband used to say, triumphantly, "Three points!" when he made a basket, a habit that our sons and I picked up. Inevitably, though, a time comes when the successful baskets become fewer and fewer. Whether it's your aim or your arm, that crumpled piece of refuse, instead of landing where it should, bounces off the rim and necessitates a bend. Even standing over the wastepaper basket doesn't always work; fully a third of the time, my hand mysteriously gives a little twist, sending a tissue awry to hit the rim and land on the floor.

I dare not complain, as well-meaning friends often reply, in concerned tones, "Do you have help?" I tell them my cleaning man comes every two weeks. "Yes," they say, "but how are you managing?" What—I'm going to hire someone to hang around in case my sweater falls on the floor or my purse tips over?

Why do these things happen that never happened when we were younger? Is there an answer?

Once in a while I still have to use a pen, perhaps to write a check or maybe even (how retro!) to send a personal note to someone. I sign my name and put the pen down. Need I tell you what happens? Of course, it rolls onto the floor. Pencils are sometimes made with flat sides that I assume are meant to keep them from rolling, but they often do anyway. So much for that invention. Pens are another story. In the olden days pens had clips, and in fact some still do. But how many of them, especially if one leaves off the cap, are simply narrow cylinders just waiting to roll?

On reflection, I think I've solved the mystery. Things always fell on the floor; it's just harder to pick them up now. My son suggests I get a robot, or invent one. Daily, it seems, humans are finding new uses for artificial intelligence and robotic creatures. There are robots that clean the floor; why not one that picks up fallen objects? I picture something along the lines of C3PO, a benevolent-looking creature that responds to commands, small enough to reach the floor easily but tall enough to present me with the retrieved object. About the size of a fire hydrant.

What is it with these things? Is it that somebody up there just wants us to get our exercise? Perhaps a higher power is making sure that we get in a bend or two every day. I feel so much better for having figured that out. Now, at least when I swear as I bend, I will know to whom I am swearing, and for whom the pen rolls.

Unsolicited Advice From Well-Meaning Friends

IN THE SCHEME OF THINGS, I haven't been a widow for very long. It's amazing what you can learn in a short time, especially when you have few options. If you're not the family bill-payer, for example, you become one—unless you are my mother-in-law, who solved that problem by having her son visit every Friday without fail to handle the task. I usually joined him there, even when the kids were babies and I had to struggle getting the carriage in and out of the car. If nothing else, it came with a really good dinner.

In addition to learning new and often undesired skills, I became the object, not only of sympathy, but of an abundance of well-meaning but sometimes misguided advice. I felt like Benjamin, in *The Graduate*, who is accosted at his college graduation party by a man who has just one thing to say: "Plastics." In my own case, the advisors generally had a few more words than that, starting at the *Shiva*, or Jewish days of condolence following a death.

"No big decisions." Generally, these advisors would take me aside and, after telling me that they knew it was too early to be thinking of such things, would immediately forget what they had just said and, gently or emphatically—depending on the person—tell me not to make any big decisions yet. Better to wait a year. Although I had absolutely no intention of making any major decisions regarding moving, selling, buying, even traveling, until a fair amount of time had passed, my response was generally, "Thank you. I think you're right, and I do plan to wait before doing anything." However, why a year is the magic time period is open to question.

My closest friend, Stef, a widow for fifteen years, gave people the dolorous news that *the second year is worse than the first.* No doubt for her it was. But she didn't say that it was worse for *her*; she implied that it was universally worse. One friend (female) found this information very helpful; another (male) was horrified at the thought. It turned out he didn't have to worry; by year two he was safely ensconced in the arms of a girlfriend who, with astonishing skill and timing, had pounced on him at five months. I couldn't predict, but I didn't want to dread year two because of Stef's experience. I told her so, and she modified her spiel. As it turned out, for me, the second year wasn't much different from the first. Over time the pervasive loneliness has gotten worse, but the raw emptiness has mostly faded, except when a random comment or event triggers an occasional reappearance for which you are totally unprepared.

Opposite are those advisors who kept telling me that I just had to bear getting through a year of "firsts," with the implication that I would feel less devastated on my second wedding anniversary alone, or my second Thanksgiving or Hanukah. I don't foresee a day when my anniversary, which is also the summer solstice, will become just another day to cross off the calendar.

I'm told that some people react to grief by overeating, and others do the reverse. I'd intentionally lost eighteen pounds before my widowhood, but then another fifteen melted away. I was quite slender at the weight I'd been at my wedding, though the disappeared fat left my skin hanging in unflattering ways. Things sag. An old friend, Carol, was very concerned about my weight loss. "What does the doctor say?" she demanded. When I told her the doctor was delighted, she decided he was wrong. "You're too thin! You have to eat!" she said firmly. In truth, my appetite is not what it was. Still, it's my business, not hers. Somewhat to my relief, it was discovered that an overactive thyroid had recurred. Able to blame my weight loss on something besides lack of eating, she finally backed off—until I was having lunch at her apartment one day and didn't consume enough tuna fish to satisfy her. When she reached across the table, grabbed my plate and tried to put more food on it after I had declined seconds, I practically yelled, "Stop!" and she did, but reluctantly. Even now, after having gained back several pounds, every time I see her, she looks at me appraisingly. As it happens, her husband died just three months prior to mine, and I have never checked out her weight or otherwise thought about her condition. I don't know if I am less caring or less intrusive.

On the subject of my general well-being, my sons and their wives—all lovely and with my best interests at heart (as well as their need not to worry about me)—sat me down for a pow-wow. I had perhaps made the mistake of venting my frustrations about my arthritic limitations—a lack of dexterity that Howard's help had disguised in the past—and also how I had no interest whatsoever in cooking. "You've got to get help," they said. At least they didn't suggest I move to a retirement community, not even that I get a "fallen and can't get up" bracelet, though that will probably come next. One of my daughters-in-law even enlisted the assistance of my kindly neighbor, who knows everyone in the community, to find me some help. That effort resulted, for a start, in my being able to text them or another neighbor, and they or their teenagers come right over to open things for me—a great help, I admit. I call them my elves.

"You shouldn't depend on your kids." I've heard this line a lot. Sometimes I've even said it, for, with one son living four hours away and the other and his wife truly buried in work, I hesitate to call upon them too often. Yet I crave

my sons' company, and only one is nearby. The other has no room in his house for me; while it was fine to stay in a hotel when there were two of us, I'm not ready to do that alone—though I thought nothing of being alone in a hotel when my husband was home and I could call to say goodnight. The first time I was away with my son Ed and his family, I almost cried when the hotel desk clerk assigned me a room on a different floor from theirs. I hated watching them walk off together while I was alone, so I requested a room near them, which made them ever so slightly cringe. It wasn't rational but it still made me feel better. Secretly, I'd have loved adjoining rooms, but I didn't want to look like a baby or, worse, a fragile old lady. Now, having traveled with them a few times, proximity is much less of an issue, though I still prefer it.

"Think seriously about moving to an apartment." That was my sister, who said this with love and concern. She was responding to my early fear that my chest pains and shortness of breath were a heart attack. (They weren't.) Howard and I had been looking at apartments and planned to get serious about moving after his surgery and recovery—best-laid plans that were not to be—and I still had that intention. But not for another year or more—big decisions and all that. Ultimately, I could not rid myself of a vision in which my kids would help me pack and unpack, put away all my worldly goods for me, do all they could to help me get settled in, at which point they would leave, the door would close, and I would want nothing more than to jump

out the window. I decided to remain in my house for a while.

"Never say no to an invitation" is practically a mantra among us widows, for if you decline an invite, you may not receive any in the future. Another, which I also endorse, is, "Always pay your own way if you're with a couple." My mother-in-law had a variation on that. Although I believe she did pay, she also invited couples to partake of her housekeeper's sumptuous and scrumptious meals, an invitation they eagerly accepted.

"Keep busy!" is the idea. As a widow, try keeping busy on a weekend, when families and couples are enjoying their time together and flaunting it on Facebook for us to envy. I am of a generation of girls most of whom were mortified if we lacked a Saturday night date; we hate seeing a movie alone, even on weekdays. We slink into our seats, hoping not to run into anyone, much as if we're doing something illicit. Even the shyest among us sometimes steel ourselves and call people about seeing a movie, especially other widows or otherwise single friends. We're grateful when others call—someone wants to spend time with us! And we are overwhelmed with gratitude if it's a couple or, best of all, our children who want to get together.

Keeping busy also gets tougher in the summer, when families, couples, and even single close friends have plans they've followed for many years, just as my husband and I did. Courses we take to fill our days are finite, and usually on hiatus in summer. Everyone seems to have a need to take time off in summer, including the therapists who might help us as we frantically try to create a structure for our lives and eagerly await September. Then what? The dreaded *isolation* returns. Isolation knows no economic or sociological boundaries; it's awful for everyone. I've certainly found myself on the edge of the abyss when I've had too many days alone. One solution: find other widows in the same boat. In fact, try *boarding* a boat with them on a terrific cruise, if you aren't subject to seasickness.

And how many times have I been told to *"Try new things."* Stef, who is descended from a long line of nonreligious socialists, even joined Hadassah, a Jewish women's organization—surely a desperate move on her part. I, the proud daughter of a woman who founded her Hadassah chapter, could more readily see me doing that—but it's not for me (or for her, in truth). Stef also took up bridge, which she now teaches, and mah jongg, which she played as a young mother. Nope. I can't help it; I picture my aunt at her country club playing mah jongg with her cronies, all wearing brightly colored Capri pants, their hair carefully coiffed. I cannot overcome that image, even knowing that it's a challenging game played by Asian men. I may—given my own occasional desperation—take bridge lessons. After all, if I'm going to have some old-lady social capital, I probably should learn one such skill.

"Go out on dates" is probably the new thing that's most fraught. Hah! If you're a woman, it's also all too unlikely. My friend Larry, I heard, told his wife Marsha, "Jackie will

be alright. She's smart, she's good-looking, and she's rich." Two of those comments are exaggerations. I leave it to you to figure out which, but hearing his appraisal of my chances warmed my heart. Opposing his view is, "Isn't it too soon for you to date?" asked by none other than this same Larry. How would he know? People past a certain age don't worry about "too soon." We live in a world of *carpe diem.*

And so I hike along as life, like artificial turf, rolls out before me. This is the first time in my life that I've been a single adult. I'm not crazy about any of it, except for being accountable to no one but me and being able to go to sleep with a book and phone on the bed. There's no one to say, "You're still up?" "You're still on the phone?" I admit it—I love the freedom despite the loneliness.

I'm deeply grateful to all my advisors, but I do wish sometimes that they would refrain. That is, except for one: my dear Howard, who always said: "Don't anticipate." As I nervously await medical test results or wonder despite my bravado how I'll get through holidays and special occasions, those two words remain the best advice I've ever received. Thanks, Babe.

Goodbye, Old Car—Time to Move On

ONE DAY I HAD A BRIEF RESPITE between a doctor and trainer appointment, an hour in which there was not enough time to do anything of substance and too much to go directly to the next destination. So I stopped at home, pulling my Nissan SUV into the garage. As I was about to head upstairs, I remembered a call I had to make, so I did it from the car, on my cell phone. I then checked emails, responded to a few and, without realizing it, dozed off in the car for a few minutes. When I awoke, it was time to head to the workout.

Deciding to run inside for a quick bathroom break before leaving, I opened the car door. I heard a gradually weakening clicking sound. The windshield wipers started slowly and spookily swishing back and forth. The ceiling lights blinked intermittently and wearily, like a sick person just waking up.

I tried to start the car. Nothing but a dashboard light or two. I had turned off the car when I drove into the garage, yet after thirty minutes I had a seemingly dead battery.

My reflexive thought was that I'd ask Howard to call AAA while I took his car to the trainer. Then I remembered: Howard was dead. I had turned in his leased Lincoln a month before. There was nobody to deal with this but me. I called, and a mechanic arrived.

The battery had a charge, but even the mechanic couldn't start the ignition. He speculated that there was some kind of short circuit in the system, but he couldn't tow the car because, as an All-Wheel-Drive vehicle, it needed a flatbed truck. Who knew? He left, and I called AAA again for a flatbed. About half an hour later it showed up, driven by the same guy. I went into the house to get my phone charger. When I came back, the mechanic said, "You're not going to believe this." The car had started. He assured me I could drive because the problem had happened when I stopped the car. With trepidation I drove to the Nissan dealership, and this is what I was told: By my sitting in the car and not opening the door and getting out, the computer was still running, and it drained the battery. In other words, if I were to pick someone up at a railroad station, and the train was delayed half an hour, and I turned off the motor and sat in the car, the battery would drain. That's about as plausible as an incident a few years ago, when I got out of the car for twenty minutes and the battery went dead. I was then told that it'd died because I'd left the radio on when turning off the motor. Yeah, right.

I left the car with Nissan for a checkup, after learning that my warranty had—of course—just expired. They were to call me in the morning with a diagnosis. At a prior Nissan diagnosis adventure, the clock had kept mysteriously resetting itself to exactly five hours and ten minutes early. That time they'd told me they couldn't fix the clock and would have to replace the entire electrical system for $3,800. I had kept the broken clock.

This time, Nissan never called at all. I tried them around 1:30, only to be told, "The gentleman working on your car went home sick. He has terrible allergies, and I've been left with all these cars to repair, and I can't get to all of them—"

I stopped him. No patience. At wits' end, I said, "My husband is dead, so I can top your tale of woe. What's the deal with my car?" When I heard that they'd "try to look at it tomorrow," I decided to pick up the car and take my chances as I shopped for new wheels. As I'd expected, the mechanic hadn't been able to replicate the dead motor. Of course, they'd been trying to do that while driving it, which is not when the problem occurred.

So long, Nissan. I have neither the time nor the patience to handle a fraught relationship with an automobile. Time for a new car. I'm filled with dread. Widowhood means learning about a lot of new things. Some are very interesting; some you'd rather not know. This was somewhere in between. But a new journey was about to begin.

Car Virgin No More

SOMEWHAT TO MY SURPRISE, I recently leased a Lexus. I, who had grown up with Chevys and Fords, had always thought Lexi a bit pretentious, until I fell in love with one.

And I did this—my first solo car acquisition—by myself. Of course, it was not actually my first; with my father as advisor and co-signer, I'd purchased a car when I was not quite twenty-one and starting my first real job. I'd conscientiously made payments until I married, a year later. Then my husband paid off the rest, as most nice husbands did in those days.

After that early experience, any time either of us needed new wheels, the other went along. Looking at cars was like a game—sitting in them, peeking in the trunk, kicking the tires (Why do we do that?), selecting a color. At age fifty, Howard bought his first luxury model, a Lincoln Town Car.

As comfortable and well-upholstered as a sofa, it felt as though we were driving around in our living room.

I had some interesting experiences with his car. Once, when mine was in the shop, I drove the Town Car to a meeting. As I was leaving, a friend of ours—male, of course—said, "Howard lets you drive that?" *Lets me!?* Ironically, as this friend is a decade older than I am, he's been my passenger a couple of times. Another time, when I parked it in the economy car-filled lot of the nonprofit where I worked, the executive director only half-jokingly asked me if it came with a little chauffeur's cap. Speaking of which, Howard once was picking me up from a fundraiser at a posh Upper East Side address. I was wearing a long fur coat. The doorman, seeing a Town Car drive up, opened the rear passenger door. I told him that I didn't think my husband would appreciate my sitting in back. We laughed about it for years.

After enjoying two Town Cars, Howard downsized to a smaller but still luxurious model. When he died, I turned in his car. Even now, when I see a burgundy Lincoln MKZ, I always wonder if it was Howard's. It had had two years left on its lease and about 6,000 miles on the odometer. Someone got a very good deal.

I couldn't wait to get rid of my old Nissan, with its many problems, and select something just for me. So here I was, a technical car virgin, ready to be initiated. I was excited and a little apprehensive.

My sons researched different models, especially Edward, whose first words after Mommy, Daddy and No were, "See car?" Nevertheless, I soon realized that I would have to do most of the test driving and negotiating myself—egad. I'd heard all kinds of stories about women and car salesmen, including one in which a woman asked her brother to come with her and "bring your penis." He didn't have do anything but sit there, and her treatment immediately improved.

Ed did come with me for my first test drive, in a small Honda. The salesman tended to tell me how to drive. Rather than just saying, for example, "Go straight" or "Turn right," it was more like, "After the light changes, go straight." I first thought I was imagining this; after the fourth cautionary instruction, I casually said to him, "You know, I think I was driving before you were born." Ed thought I was imagining things, but I said that, as a man, he was not sensitized to this kind of sexism and wouldn't notice it. Without a doubt, the salesman would never have spoken to him like that.

One day, when the whole process was depressing me, I decided to check out a Toyota. I combed my hair, put on lipstick, and went to a nearby agency. Both Toyota and Lexus used a gearshift that was manageable with arthritic hands. The salesman showed me a zippy electric blue Rav4. We talked some numbers, and he arranged for a test drive later that week. The following day I meandered into a Lexus agency, Toyota's more luxurious cousin, and made a similar appointment. Two days later, I test drove one car in the morning and the other in the afternoon. Both were suitable, and I adored the comfort of the Lexus.

But I faced a dilemma. Was I a Lexus kind of person? I felt as though the Toyota represented *Jackie* and the Lexus *Mrs. Guttman*—not even *Ms.* Did I want to be dignified Mrs. Guttman or fun-loving Jackie? For the first time, the decision was entirely in my hands, and it was daunting.

Then again, when had I come to believe that cars were a representation of personality types? Perhaps, then, a Lexus was in my future. To my delight, after the usual "I have to speak to my manager" dance, the Lexus salesman offered lease terms that were better than I'd anticipated. Hey, I thought, maybe this wasn't so difficult, until they tried to pressure me into driving away with the new car that very day, leaving my old Nissan behind. They said they would clean out my two cartons' worth of junk and put it in big bags for me. I could not let them do it. My husband had put almost as much mileage on the Nissan as I had. Half the junk was his. I needed to clean it out myself, not have strangers do it. I needed to talk to it, to explain to Howard what I was doing, and to say goodbye to the car that had been a part of our life together. "Hell," I said to myself, "it's only a car, and I don't even like it that much," but I was compelled to do it my way. That evening, I determinedly and slightly tearfully cleaned out the Nissan.

The next morning, as arranged, I showed up at the showroom at 9:30 sharp. The salesman asked if I'd like to see my new car before we finished signing everything. We had done a lot of the paperwork, and he'd dealt with my insurance company the previous day. We went onto the lot and, to my astonishment and utter dismay, the car was the wrong color, silver gray instead of the far more elegant graphite shade that I'd selected. In his only truly false move, the salesman tried to convince me that I was mistaken, suggesting that perhaps I'd confused it with a used model I had first test-driven. I was infuriated. With a raised eyebrow and a firm voice, I shut him down fast, ignoring his complaints about having to redo the paperwork. That was his problem, not mine. We agreed that I would return at 3:30.

That afternoon I cautiously did so. After a small delay, I was escorted to the usual financial person. (Why do the financial folks always look slick and manicured? Is it a custom in the car industry?) I have a hand tremor that worsens when I'm agitated or nervous. I have a name that's eighteen letters long. I had to sign my name, mostly with a stylus on one of those awful digital pads, at least a dozen times. I could probably claim forgery, as the signatures don't resemble mine in the slightest.

Finally, nearly two hours later, I staggered out to the car lot, at which point I was introduced to a "technology assistant" who would explain to me how the car worked. All I wanted to do was go home. Years ago, when we'd buy me a car, the salesman would poke his head in the window, show me the ignition, and wish me well with a goodbye wave as Howard and I drove off. This orientation, however, took at least forty-five minutes, as he explained to me the triple redundancies of the navigation system, the climate control, the telephone system, the Bluetooth, the Redeye. . . . By the time he'd finished his onslaught, all I retained was how to start and stop.

I carefully drove home, introduced my new car to its garage, apologized that I hadn't swept it out—indeed, there was a lot of garbage from the old car lying around—gave it a pat, welcomed it to its new home, did everything but put out some hay and sugar cubes. Then I went upstairs and fell into bed.

I was very pleased with myself for surviving my first time. I ended up with a rather elegant automobile that I think will serve me very well. But I was immensely sad that there was no one with whom I could share the excitement of my shiny new vehicle, no one to give me a kiss and congratulate me, no one I could take out for a drive. Losing my car virginity, like its bodily counterpart, left me excited, relieved. . .and maybe just a bit let down.

Confessions of a Pet Curmudgeon

If I see one more adorable dog or, worse still, a cuddly cat on Facebook, I will scream. It's bad enough when Friends—even the ones who actually are friends—post photos of their meals or travels, but why must I admire their pets? Or even simply "like" them? And it's not necessarily their own pets—it's any dog or cat with a playful, soulful, or gleeful expression on its darling face, especially if it's a baby of the species or, God help us, is riding on the back of a larger animal. Who cares? I for one do not.

Spare me the sweet foibles of the beastly species; animal curmudgeon that I am, I prefer people. Think about it: People don't need to be walked or their poop scooped; they don't require litter boxes that someone must empty. They can *tell* you what they want or don't want. Animals, on the other hand, demand high maintenance, to put it politely.

Of course, people can as well, but I don't have to put up with them. I can walk away.

Consider a dog. You want to go for a walk, and it immediately assumes it's joining you. It leaps into the air with unbridled glee, and if you dare to start leaving without it, it stares glumly at you with pathetically sad eyes, hoping to manipulate you into giving in. If you weaken, it forces you to walk at its pace and stop when it has to sniff, pee, or worse. And if you encounter another dog, be prepared for growls, pulls on the leash that can knock you off your own two feet, and barks and leaps that preclude any conversation with the other dog's equally beleaguered owner—or shall we say master? Ha! Who really is the master here? Does the dog serve the master, or the master serve the dog? Then there is the sniffing. What is it about dogs' rear quarters that is so overwhelmingly tempting to other dogs? How can any civilized being take pleasure in such behavior? Disgusting!

Not to be ignored is the feeding issue. Unlike people, who can open the refrigerator and make a sandwich, the dog pines and whines if you—the master, remember—forget to put those mysterious brown pellets in the cute little bowl decorated with paw prints or refill the water bowl that, often as not, they knock over, getting your floor all wet.

And we can't forget about the danger issue. Some people get a dog for protection, to make their lives safer. How safe is it to be out walking the beast on a dark winter night? If someone comes at you, is your adorable little cavadoodle going to transform itself into White Fang and go on the attack to save your life? Will he—or she, of course—run for help like Rin-Tin-Tin, barking and tugging at a police officer's sleeve so effectively that said officer will come to your rescue in the nick of time?

Speaking of danger, how about the sock toys and bone hunks that, camouflaged on your Oriental carpet, lie in wait to trip you? And if you find that you've fallen and can't get up, what's your doggie going to do about it? Probably cuddle up next to you and go to sleep. Yet this same creature, just when you want it to stay asleep in its corner, carries on like a lunatic when a friend comes to visit. It jumps, barks incessantly, and makes it virtually impossible for you to greet your guest. And if that guest backs off in horror, the dog-lover says, "Oh, he's just friendly. He's showing that he likes you! Don't back away, because he thinks that means you want to play. Oh, you don't like to be licked? Down, Fido! No, no, Jackie doesn't like you, so leave her alone." As if that does any good. Finally, with a look that can only be described as hang-dog, the master drags the dog into the bedroom and firmly closes the door, clearly thinking that the fault lies with you, the "dog bigot."

I first heard the term "dog bigot" when my sister, who worshipped her dog, could not understand why I did not. In truth, many people secretly hated this dog—a dog of divorce, high strung and unmanageable, craving attention. Rarely groomed, he had an excess of hair that hung from face to tail that hid a fairly skinny, normal-sized dog who appeared to be big and fat. This dog smelled, had a piercing bark, scratched incessantly, knocked objects off coffee tables, and generally repelled people even usually friendly to pets. It got to the point that I instantly developed asthma the moment I was in a room with it.

And don't get me started on cats. Cat-lovers say that if you want a beautiful pet that minds its own business and doesn't annoy, felines are the way to go. I admit that their faces are appealing, albeit inscrutable. If dogs manipulate people with facial expressions, cats scare us with their very lack thereof.

Cats, unlike dogs, can be left alone with a quantity of food that they somehow know how to ration over a few days. They don't bark, and their meows have a far lower decibel count—unless they are on the prowl, of course. Sounds good, but they are *sneaky*. A non-cat lover can be sitting on a sofa minding her own business when the kitty shoots up over her shoulder, landing on the back cushion and scaring the wits out of the poor visitor. The thing with a cat is that you don't have any hint of when and where it will strike, so you must remain vigilant at all times, never daring to relax into that sofa. As you sit, tensely upright, the cat-lover says, "Oh! Isn't Snookie adorable? You just never know what she will do next—she loves to keep us guessing." Sometimes Snookie or other similarly foolishly named felines will opt to leap onto your lap, claws digging into your thighs. Apparently, de-clawing has gone out of style, in order to enable the cats to protect themselves. But who will protect us, the cat curmudgeons.

Then there is that litter box. I have a friend who was so enamored of cats (and dogs) that she kept a couple despite being allergic to them. To make matters worse, she put the litter box (a euphemism that leaves me cold—it's a toilet, folks!) in the guest bathroom. If I was her house guest and needed to use the bathroom during the night, as often as not I'd have to stifle a scream when I saw two eyes peering out from under the sink and realized I was interrupting Fluffy doing her business. If the cat had finished, I found my slippers—or even, heaven help me, my feet—crunching through crumbly stuff on the floor. Truly nauseating.

My late husband always loved children and animals, and they returned his affection. I knew this well before we were married, and I even warned him that, were we to wed, there would be no pets. He married me anyway, telling me years later that he thought I would change my mind—foolish man.

The closest we came to having a pet was a goldfish. When my younger son Marc was about six, he came to me at a school fair to ask if he could try a ring-toss game for which the prize was a fish. Marc had minor neurological issues and, in consequence, was not a very well-coordinated child; he also had a stammer. Wanting to motivate him, I said it was fine with me. He was thrilled, running to my husband and crying, "D-Daddy! Mommy said I could have a g-goldfish!" He was irresistible, so that when he did indeed win that fish, off we went, goldfish in baggie, to buy a bowl and some accoutrements.

Some time later, when one day the fish was drifting sluggishly around the bowl almost belly-up, I put in fresh water and then ran to the pet store and got some medicinal drops. To everyone's astonishment, mine most of all, the fish revived, living for another couple of years. That's about as close as I've ever gotten to taking care of a pet. After all, as the fish didn't bark, jump on me, or lick, how could I not have a measure of affection for it?

All this pet hostility changed, I now must admit, when my grand-dog Clayton came into our lives. When my son Edward sent us a photo of their newly acquired puppy, a few months old, I unexpectedly fell in love. Clayton looked like a toy, with caramel-colored curls, floppy ears, and round dark button eyes. He is a mix of poodle and King Charles cavalier spaniel, which is the kind of fact I would never before have remembered about an animal. For our first meeting, I bought him a dog toy; I was possessed.

A decade later, the curls have faded some, but he has a dignified demeanor and a beautiful profile while retaining his playful nature and ability to levitate straight up when excited. I call him my favorite grandchild, as he pays more attention to me than the human ones do. My grandchildren walk him, as I'm still not into scooping poop, but when I stay with them, I give the dog food, water, and an occasional treat, and so he has become my pal.

With the loss of my husband, Clayton has come to play

an additional role. If I'm feeling sad and lonely, I'm not averse to giving myself a bit of pet therapy. I invite him onto the sofa, where he cuddles up beside me and practically purrs when I pet him. I practically purr back. And I swear that, when he turns and looks at me, he is smiling.

But please don't tell anyone. I have a reputation to maintain.

Special

IT'S A TOUGH TIME IN THE YEARLY CYCLE. A year ago, my husband was struggling to recover from the after-effects of major surgery. Sadly, after eight weeks, he died of too many complications to enumerate or overcome. He was a brave and kind man, big and strong.

Like so many otherwise competent and confident widows, I found myself surprised, indeed stunned, bewildered, and intermittently angry. And lonely. Of course loneliness goes with the territory, yet I feel it so much more now, though I've been living on my own for just over a year. On the surface, at least, I'm like all the other seventy-plus widows, going to concerts, movies, and museums with my terrific female friends or the occasional otherwise unavailable male, but "standard widowhood" was not how it was supposed to be. It feels all wrong.

My sister and I were brought up to be special. My

mother disparaged people by saying they were ordinary, or common, though economically we were a bit south of middle class and educationally would be the first to graduate from college. But whatever we may have lacked, my mother instilled in us the idea that we were not like other people; we were a cut above. She succeeded. To this day my sister and I feel that we are somehow different—yes, even a little better than some. While we love and value our friends, to some degree we are both loners.

Ethically, my parents were at the top of the heap. We were brought up to be well-mannered, self-sufficient, considerate of others, and, when confronted by difficult situations, to reflect and then do the right thing. Though my mother was a swearer and smacker, neither she nor my father ever used a racial or religious epithet; it simply was not part of their, or our, vocabulary. We brought up our children the same way, as they are raising theirs.

Cultivating being different had a downside. My mother had a thing about arriving late to parties; she thought it was important to "make an entrance." Consequently, as adults, we had to train ourselves to be punctual. Perhaps the worst part was that, at a time when conformity was everything, we never looked quite like the other kids. In junior high, for example, along with circular felt "poodle skirts" and crinolines, pastel-colored leather jackets—turquoise, pink, lavender—were the rage. My jacket was brown. Never would she have me look like everyone else. We were special. As most of my wardrobe was handed down from a cousin to my sister to another cousin and, finally, to me, I was rarely in style in any case. Even my Girl Scout uniform was out of date.

For better and worse, the sense of not being run-of-the-mill never left me. And so it was that, when I became a widow, I didn't think that my experience would parallel other women's. As my loving and comfortable marriage had not precluded a mild flirtation now and then, I did not anticipate that, nearly a year after my husband's death, I would feel, and be, so solitary. In my naivete I even thought that one old friend, now a widower, would turn to me, as his fondness for me had always been evident. But no, he is content with his younger, healthier girlfriend. She has brought him a new life and new friends. Best of all for him is that there is no residual guilt, as he had not known her when his wife was alive. I, on the other hand, am a remembrance of things past; he might see a relationship with me as a kind of betrayal. Or perhaps he just thinks she's sexier. And so I'm left, one of the thundering herd of aging widows patrolling every suburban community. We take classes and do good works—in packs, it sometimes seems.

I had thought that my widowhood would be more cosmopolitan, that, when I chose to, I would have a man beside me at the theater, across from me at the restaurant, and, now and then, next to me in my bed. But it didn't work out that way. For the first time in my life, I felt ordinary.

Hope Springs Eternal

FIVE MONTHS AFTER my husband's death, I began window-shopping—fooling around on on-line dating sites. Too soon, some friends thought, but what did they know? I wasn't planning to be alone for long. How naive I was.

Overnight, I started receiving at least sixteen photos and profiles daily. It was almost fun, seeing who was out there. I noticed that most men who were attractive to me were Jewish, from New York City, or both, so when I finally took a serious plunge, it was on a site for Jewish singles. Perhaps because of the relatively small older-male single Jewish population, every day would bring me the same five men—at least I think they were men—one photo looked like a snake. His secret personality?

There was, however, a larger problem. To a man, each of the responders was seeking a woman eight to twenty years younger than he was—or than I am. I emailed the site to ask where the older men were for *me*. Apparently, its practice is to look at my preferences when making matches, not those of the guys. As a woman in her middle seventies, I had asked for men aged sixty-eight to eighty, but true to what I'd heard, ninety percent of Jewish men in that age bracket want young chicks. When the site sent me a photo of a woman, I was finished. I canceled my subscription.

I next tried Match. As the largest dating app, it seemed likely to have the largest pool of men. In the first few weeks, several men "viewed" me, and I did hear from a few. Some were semi-literate; one wanted someone to drive cross-country with him; others were simply creepy. As bad as this was, it was an improvement on the responses my daughter-in-law's mother had received: nothing.

I then discovered Sy451. He was interested only in a casual relationship, which suited me, as the craving I'd had for strong male arms around me had settled into a dull ache. His profile was long but not verbose; he wrote well; he had a sense of humor; his smile was pleasant. I contacted him. He confessed that he was temporarily out of commission due to a setback following hip-replacement surgery. I told him not to worry as I have artificial knees. I suggested that, if he was bored while convalescing, he was welcome to write. Two weeks later I heard from him; he was functional once again. Because we live about forty miles apart, we decided to meet midway for lunch.

On the big day, despite my intention not to stake anything on the meeting, I changed my outfit twice. In my black Eileen Fisher slacks, violet sweater, and artfully tied scarf, I looked boring even to me. And my normally curly hair was drooping sadly. As I crossed the Tappan Zee Bridge to meet Sy451, I felt as though I were auditioning. For what, I wondered: a tryst with a retired math teacher with a new hip?

When I entered the crowded restaurant, a woman said, "Husband?" I hadn't heard that in a long time.

Startled, I said, "No, uh, a man." She pointed toward a table in the back. I was very nervous until he knocked over a glass of ice water as he rose to greet me. I couldn't resist. I said, "Talk about an ice-breaker!" and found someone to clean it up. But he didn't laugh, which was disappointing.

Sy451 was wearing jeans and a not-new shirt and sweater—not especially designed to impress. As I tried to figure out what I could order that would minimize my arthritic eating difficulties, we talked fairly comfortably of grandchildren, art, and music, central to both our families. As we ate, now and then bits of food got caught in his short beard. When a dab of yogurt landed on his cheek, my eyes, laser-like, kept going to that spot. I couldn't stand it; I finally gently informed him of its presence. He wiped it away with thanks, following that with a story about a woman with whom he'd had lunch who never told him about the egg in his beard. He referred to her as a bitch, which startled me. I suspect she was just embarrassed. What should she have said: "Hey, buddy, you have egg on your face"?

I wondered why a decent, intelligent, mostly well-mannered man was still hanging loose eight years after the death of his wife. It certainly couldn't be the food-in-beard problem. Whatever his story, my reaction to him was "meh." He paid for lunch; he drove me to my distantly parked car in his extraordinarily messy one; he thanked me for coming across the bridge to meet him. But as my then-single son used to say, "there was nothing there."

I decided to wait a day or two before telling him thanks but no thanks, but he beat me to it. I received a polite text saying that I'm a nice woman but he didn't think it was a good fit. I texted back, thanking him for lunch and telling him that I agreed. I added that perhaps I am a nice woman, but that didn't begin to describe me. I wished he could have met the wiseass, irreverent, jeans and t-shirt me. The adventurer who, while her family took vacation tennis lessons, made a foray into the nude Jacuzzi instead, who sat there in the bubbles making conversation with a man who, coincidentally, had been my son's friend's soccer coach, while simultaneously thinking, "My god, we're naked!"

Sy451 texted again. He'd discovered to his dismay that the restaurant had given me his leftover sandwich. Poor guy, he'd paid for lunch and all he'd gotten was my wilted salad. I sympathized, wishing him a Happy Thanksgiving. He returned my wishes, and that was that. Months later I tried to fix him up with a friend who is a retired science teacher and an artist, but by this time I had revised my profile, making it a tad more titillating. Sy had no interest in my friend but did want to see me again. I didn't follow up. Sometimes I wish I had.

I learned that, compared to some of the horror stories about on-line dating, like the guy who, a minute or two after meeting, told my friend of a friend that he likes blow jobs, I'd done pretty well. Nevertheless, after a few forays into this world, I cancelled Match.com. I discovered that I wanted to meet someone in person, to feel the small but delicious thrill of knowing that you've clicked. In fact, I've had that experience a couple of times, but unless their wives leave them or leave this earth, nothing will come of it. Still, just knowing that there are men who find me attractive or interesting sustains me, for a while. It makes me feel good. It makes me feel special.

The months passed. I found myself stalking men in the grocery store, the gym, even the bank. Is he wearing a wedding ring? Well groomed? Friendly? Tall? I learned that there's a crucial window for the hunt, after the wife has died but before other women have staked their claim; however, I haven't figured out the finer points of this strategy. When do I pounce? And how do I go about it? And where is the sweet spot between pouncing and invisibility? My obsession with finding someone, just to share dinner or a movie, was getting out of hand. Clearly, the odds of stumbling onto a good prospect were slim. I've never known how to flirt skillfully, not in my teens or in my seventies. I could be flirtatious when I was married; knowing that my husband was in the wings gave me confidence. I had no stake in whether the guy would flirt back, but now, any future coupling is riding on it.

A year later, with a significant birthday looming, I decided to give my search another shot while I was still under a certain age. I changed my ID name from Jax—too tomboyish?—to the more feminine (and French!) Jacqueline. According to Match, I was getting "viewed" a fair amount, approved of fairly often, but in this round I was contacted only once, by Jerry.

Jerry was a semi-retired psychotherapist. He messaged me that I was attractive and my profile engaging—things every woman looking online wants to hear. He lived in the city, another plus. We had a brief conversation and then arranged to meet for coffee.

I agreed so quickly because it was evident that he was having difficulty hearing me on the phone. He attributed that to my cell phone but, having had a husband who was significantly deaf, I had little doubt that he had a major hearing issue. That was okay, I figured, because if we were sitting face-to-face it shouldn't be a problem. I was wrong.

I walked into the Carnegie Cup Café on East Eighty-eighth and Park. He stood up to greet me. I could see immediately that he was too small for me, about my height and kind of wiry. No bulk. The shop had a few tables and a counter at which you could pick up coffee, sandwiches, and pastries. I grabbed an iced cappuccino and a chocolate chip cookie for $7.35. It occurred to me that it would have been nice if he'd stood up and asked what he could get me instead of pointing me in the direction of the counter. I had, after all, paid the George Washington Bridge toll and taken a crosstown cab. All right, I figured, he's cheap. But, as older single men are a scarce commodity, I didn't want to write him off immediately. I decided not to rush to judgment.

Sounding like the therapist he was, he started interrogating me. I noted that he had a photo and profile of me that were not from Match. I asked where he'd gotten them. LinkedIn. Ah, I'd forgotten about that. We talked or, rather, he asked questions, and I answered them. Then I asked him some questions, reminding myself to be a dutiful and attentive listener. Every question I asked, he couldn't hear, and I finally gave up after asking him about his alma mater, New York University, three separate times, even carefully over-articulating "Neuw Yorrk Yuniversity." As I have degrees from NYU, I thought it might provide some common ground, but, alas, NYU did not make it past his hearing aids. Although he had a habit of frequently returning to the same topics, I excused that. We were trying to get to know each other. He focused on three subjects: East Meadow High School, Wave Hill (my former place of employment), and his childhood in Princeton.

Our appointment had been for 3:30. He'd asked if I could get there at 3:00, and I'd told him no, but that 3:30 would work. As it happened, I showed up about 3:15 to find him already sitting there. Perhaps he'd never heard the exchange regarding my arrival time. At approximately 3:50, commenting that forty-five minutes had passed—the equivalent of a therapy session, he said—he abruptly informed me that he had to be on his way. He stood up, wished me luck, and off he marched, leaving me sitting there with an empty cappuccino cup in front of me. I had wasted three hours and forty dollars to spend forty-five minutes with a deaf guy who was too short and too old though chronologically younger. He, meanwhile, had walked three or four blocks from his apartment.

I was livid. I felt impotent and infuriated. When I got home, I did the only thing I could do: I found the exchange of online messages between us. I sent him a last message. I told him that if he actually wanted to meet a woman rather than just being an annoyance, he should get new hearing aids because he'd missed half of what I was saying to him. I added, "And you are cheap." Not very satisfying.

Because we women fasten on perceived imperfections in our looks or build, I also took a good look in the mirror. I looked just fine. Then came the "What I should have said" stage. I should have said, "Sit down! We may not have any interest in one another. I certainly have no interest in you. You are too short, too old, and too deaf. You talked *at* me, in part because you didn't even hear what I was saying. You should have bought me my coffee, if for no reason other than you walked three blocks to get here and I drove ten miles, paid a toll, and took a cab. You owe me more than forty minutes of your precious time, but I'm not interested in taking payment. Now get the hell out of here!"

I couldn't get past my rage. The next day, having learned his last name during our non-conversation, I googled him and found four reviews from his therapy patients. Sample comments:

He doesn't listen, at all! I had to repeat myself many, many times. . . . I would not recommend.

Very weird experience—he's pretty much a jerk. Do not go here.

He constantly focused on things that were irrelevant. . .if anything it made me feel worse than when I first started seeing him.

I was thrilled. To use psycho-speak, I felt validated. Only then could I dismiss him from my mind. At last it came to me that the real source of my anger was—again—the difference between widows and widowers: When they are ready, most men will find women, either through friends eager to fix them up or, yes, online. Women, on the other hand, rarely are introduced to men; we often have to wait to be found, and going online becomes our only recourse.

Am I desperate or optimistic? I don't know, but please excuse me. I just got a message from Arnie. Could he be the one? Hope springs eternal.

Snowstorm Blues

IT WASN'T SO LONG AGO that a major snowstorm was fun, an adventure. Not the fun of when we were children, breathlessly awaiting the moment we could go outside and play in the snow, but the pre-pandemic novelty of being cooped up together, unable or unwilling to brave the ice and cold but reveling in the change of pace, the enforced togetherness, and the permission that inclement weather gives us to accomplish very little.

It's different now, in the late winter following my husband's death. As I sit alone in our home, hoping that the old-growth trees outside won't fall on the power lines or, worse, on the roof, I feel empty. The beautiful crystalline snow, normally a source of wonder that makes me smile in spite of myself, has become the enemy. Being snowed in is only fun with company.

When you live alone, no matter how much you enjoy

your own company or appreciate peace and solitude, being prevented by the elements from going outdoors leaves you lethargic and lonely. The lack of stimulation sends me back in time, recalling snowy days of snuggling under the covers with a long, enveloping, and warm body, a body that belonged to a gentle someone who loved me. In those days, when I remembered to do it and Howard opened the flue for me, I'd light a fire in the fireplace I'd always coveted and then kept forgetting about. Today I envision myself sitting before crackling flames with a good book, but sharing the fire was more than half the pleasure. And even though my husband was afraid to light a fire, I'm afraid to do it without him standing there keeping a nervous eye on things.

I make a call or two, text my sons, and if the telephone rings I leap to answer it, too often finding myself listening to an advertising robot. One friend calls to check up on me, and I'm immensely grateful. I love my sons dearly, but I swear that, if I had daughters, they'd call. One son just spent a few days here with his family, and that was, as always, a welcome and wonderful change of pace, including the nutritious and tasty meals cooked by my daughter-in-law. (I'll bet she called her mother, who lives only half an hour away from her.) My other son called yesterday, and we had a great conversation. Remembering myself at their ages, I'm sure they feel that the recent visit and phone call have given them a few extra credits in the be-kind-to-mother bank. So am I an ingrate for wishing they'd have also called today, just to see how I'm doing? I think not.

Then again, if they did call to check, would I accuse them of treating me like an old lady?

Surely these feelings are not merely a function of age. When you're alone in your home after fifty-two years of sharing it with your husband, and when that home is snowed in and you're totally stuck, shouldn't your offspring intuit that it would be a mood-lifter to hear from them? No, they are busy with their families, enjoying the very same novelty that we introduced to them—playing games, watching movies, and partaking of other snowed-in adventures. I remember those days, and I want them back.

I've never had the slightest interest in living with my sons, much as I love them, their wives, and my grandchildren. They have their schedules, eating habits, and inside jokes that make up their lives. My son Ed and his family speak quietly, and I loathe having to ask them to accommodate my less than perfect ears. Also, I like my space, my privacy, and living my own life. And yet, were I with them, I could participate in Scrabble, Chinese Checkers, and other board games, read with the sound of life nearby, and sleep without being enveloped in a silence so profound that I welcome the knocking of the radiator. So I sit, trying to figure out how not to fall into the loneliness abyss, telling myself that this is the reason I may need to leave my lovely house and move to an apartment.

The doorbell rings. Who can be here in the middle of a snowstorm? I pad to the door in my slippers, open it a crack, and peek around it. Standing on my porch, swathed in parka and hood, is someone unrecognizable. I peer at him, feeling like the nasty lady whom the neighborhood kids are afraid of. He speaks. Oh, God, it's Eli, my neighbor from across the street. "We wanted to make sure you're okay and see if you need anything from the store," he says. I give him a big hug because he's giving me exactly what I need—human contact and concern. (I wonder if he has called his mother?) He's an Orthodox Jew, so I hope the hug is okay, since I'm old enough to be his mother. I tell him I'm fine but, "Thank you, thank you, thank you for thinking of me!"

After Eli leaves, I think about his visit and his words. Am I okay? *Of course I am!* It's the perpetual conflict of the aging: Why would he think I need help? And—I'm so grateful that he and his family are concerned for my well-being. The snowstorm blues are fading to bright silver. How lucky I am to have such neighbors.

"She Has a Nice Personality"—Plus Ça Change

When I was in my teens and early twenties, it was the kiss of death for a girl to be described as having a nice personality. Although it sounded like a positive attribute, everyone knew it was code for a negative: She must be homely, certainly not sexy or enticing.

I myself was probably described that way. While my face was pleasant enough, I was not especially beautiful, and with a chest that stayed washboard-like until my thirties, I would not have been described by any teenage boy as sexy. I was also too tall for most—I still am. Though I've lost a couple of inches, so have they. I did, however, have a friendly smile and that lethal nice personality. To make matters worse, I was a good girl, another death knell of desirability. I'd go to a party or a dance, dateless, and nearly always spend much of the time leaning against the wall—a classic wallflower. I tried smoking in an effort to look suave and sophisticated. Fortunately, the habit did not take hold, thanks in part to my older sister, who thought it was hilarious that her baby sibling was holding a cigarette. Not exactly the effect I was striving for.

My lack of a social life when young worked out well for the boy who became the man who became my husband, for Howard could have been described the same way. Like me, he was tall—very tall—and kind of gawky, all thick glasses and bobbing Adam's apple. When we were introduced, two shy and somewhat awkward individuals, what saved us both was that we were good dancers. People even watched us—we were graceful and well matched. We impressed onlookers into our fifties and beyond.

Initially, we shared little more than dancing. At sixteen, I had just graduated from the High School of Music and Art, and musicians were more my speed. I asked Howard if he played an instrument, and he said, "The phonograph," a feeble attempt to be funny. Forget this guy, I thought. He was just shy of his twenty-second birthday, out of college, and in the army. However, with no other prospects around for either of us, we spent some time together at the country club that his father and my uncle had helped to found. As I sat at the side of the pool, trying to look fetching in my red bathing suit, I was very impressed by the way he could dive in at one end and not come up for air until he hit the opposite wall. And he was a *nice* boy.

Through my college years we'd see each other during summers in the country and date here and there. I had boyfriends; he had girlfriends. The best way to describe what happened is that Howard lurked in the background while I grew up. The Christmas after my graduation, he proposed, and I accepted. A few months later, we were married. It was not an incandescent romance. We were not madly passionate about each other, but we were comfortable; we could always be ourselves—silly, babyish, petty—it didn't matter.

We had a good life and a lot of fun until, fifty-two years later, he left me—that is, he died. He'd had a variety of conditions and illnesses, and more than his share of surgery. He'd always come back—until he didn't, dying of a massively infected bed sore while attempting to recover from significant surgery for tongue cancer.

I am now a mature woman with a nice personality. I have other attributes, but thanks to an overactive thyroid, I've lost sufficient weight to once again almost be called gawky. Without the freshness of youth, and with the body wrinkles that occur when an older woman loses twenty-five pounds, I muse on the fact that I may never again go from being a *me* to a *we*.

Back then, when I was sixteen, I had my whole life ahead of me. There's no escaping the fact that now I have most of it behind me. Will my teenage wall-flowerhood return? Could it happen again? I know and am friends with a variety of men, married or otherwise unavailable. They enjoy talking with me. They like my sense of humor. They are intrigued that I write. Back in college, boys always liked me too, but as a friend, rarely a girlfriend, until I ensnared one, and then two, my sophomore and junior year. I may have come late to the game, but I turned out to be a pretty skilled player.

Now I'm a fairly accomplished individual, a musician, a writer. I have a lot of friends; I'm financially independent and can look elegant when I make the effort. I do have a mostly unwrinkled, fairly attractive face, and nice hair, when I remember to have it dyed on schedule. But I have no muscle tone. I have arthritically deformed and tremulous hands, artificial knees, and feet that don't match each other. I have a back studded with moles and blemishes that my doctor has called a dermatologist's dream—nightmare, more likely. How could I ever take off my clothes in front of a new man? As the time passes since my husband's death, I'm becoming increasingly aware that the likelihood of having a male companion anytime in the future is, at best, slim.

I've made brief forays onto a dating website or two. I've learned a lot, mostly not positive. I'd like to think that male values change with age, that men my age are finally interested in women with nice personalities with whom they can have fun and laugh, with whom they have a couple of interests in common. I'm sure that these men exist, but it's astonishing to most newly widowed women over the age of sixty and certainly over seventy that these beer-bellied, droopy-eyed, bald, sometimes gimpy men indicate on dating websites that the northernmost age of a potential girlfriend should be five to fifteen years younger than they are. No matter their own health status, or how they are built, most desire a woman who is "well-toned and athletic." Uh-huh. There are such women, of course, but I am by no means among them.

If I do regain the emotional stamina to venture once again onto Match or J-Date, dare I dedicate a paragraph to those annoying guys? It would go something like this:

> *Foolish men! Do you not realize that you are depriving yourselves of a kindred spirit, of love and companionship and, yes, sex, with someone for whom you need not pretend to have the virility of a stud? By this age, most women know that most men have "issues" in this department and have found ways to work around them. So don't make a certain age or a nice personality the kiss of death; rather, think of it as the kiss of life—a life that will bring you, if you let it, much happiness and contentment, even joy.*

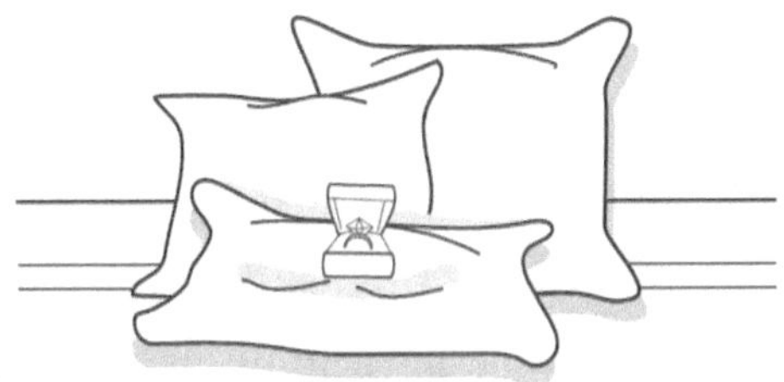

Remembrance of Rings Past

NEARLY A YEAR AFTER HOWARD DIED, I deposited my wedding and engagement rings in my bank vault. Unlike those widows who continue to wear their rings, I didn't want to present myself as married. Some women say they feel protected by their rings, as if someone is going to hit on a seventy-plus-year-old widow. It should only happen, I would sometimes think. Although I wasn't quite ready and certainly not holding my breath, I didn't want to project false impressions or create unnecessary impediments to any future efforts to meet someone. When I was ready, I wanted my availability to be clear.

Perhaps I was kidding myself, but I did hope to meet a reasonably presentable man whose company I enjoyed, with whom I could laugh and even love. Meanwhile, I had to deal with the classic dilemma of what to do with my rings. The ring dilemma was not unique to me; my bereavement group had "rolling admissions," and almost invariably the newer participants would ask, "What do you do with your rings?"

Historically, wedding rings and I have not had an exemplary relationship, largely because the minute I return home all my jewelry comes off. I've always been that way, which may account for the fact that I never wear a lot of jewelry. Earrings, wedding ring, and maybe a necklace or pin. I can be comfortable in them all day, but something about the closing of my front door triggers a "remove jewelry" reflex, and I put the ring on my dresser or night table and the other pieces wherever I keep them.

When my son Marc was about eight, he and his friend Richie were playing with clay in my bedroom. Richie's mom, an artist and sculptor and my best friend, allowed her kids to have paints and clay all over the house. The next morning I went to put on my ring. To my horror it was gone from its usual night table resting place. My stomach in knots, I retraced steps, opened drawers, looked under furniture, tore my hair trying to find that ring. It was a plain platinum band that, fourteen years earlier, had cost $50.00. I looked into replacing it and discovered that the price had soared to $350.00 (and today three times that). I figured I'd settle for the far less expensive white gold.

Ashamed of my carelessness, I was at first afraid to tell my husband it was missing. I pondered the psychological significance of the loss of the ring in which I was wed. *What did this loss say to me about the importance of my marriage?* Things like that. Perhaps I was getting melodramatic, but after more than a dozen years of marriage, I sometimes felt that we were in the doldrums. I wondered if he felt that way as well.

Suffice it to say that a few weeks later, when Richie was again visiting and his mom and I were talking in the living room, the two boys came downstairs, excitedly holding up a lump of clay. Stuck to its bottom was my wedding ring. I was too relieved and elated to wonder why they had put clay on my night table. My marriage was saved.

But most of all, I'll miss the wedding ring that I wore daily from 1989, as it has special significance, having been lost and miraculously found. After forty years of marriage, Howard lost the diamond wedding band he'd given me for our twenty-fifth anniversary. I was having my left hand x-rayed and asked him to hold the ring. His hands were so big that all he could do was slide it halfway up his pinky. The x-ray was taken; we spoke to the doctor and left. When we got home I said, "Oh, give me the ring, please," and he blanched. It was gone. I couldn't believe it and let him know exactly what I thought. I yelled; I cried; I was sarcastic; I was scathing . . .I was devastated. I called the doctor's office; there was no sign of it. They said they'd alert the cleaning staff.

Loss of the twenty-fifth anniversary ring was worse than loss of the wedding band. Platinum with two intertwined rows of intricately cut diamonds, it was stunning and unusual. More to the point, it represented one of the most romantic gestures my husband had ever made. I'd found the ring sitting on my pillow, coupled with the presentation of a plastic boat that represented the surprise cruise to Bermuda that we'd be taking to celebrate twenty-five years. Howard was not given to grand gestures, and I was simultaneously thrilled and stunned at both the ring and the trip, which he'd planned in secret with our travel agent. While I had told him of my wish for a diamond wedding ring, I'd had in mind a narrow band that we'd pick out together. This one was in another league; I was overwhelmed. I was also almost intimidated. The ring was far more elaborate than anything I could have imagined, really not my style. We even went back to the jeweler and looked at other possibilities, ultimately deciding to keep it. Somehow I would force myself to grow into it and be comfortable, and I did. It became one of my favorite pieces of jewelry.

In addition to my plain platinum marriage ring, I owned a gold band we'd bought for me on our fifth anniversary. But once I received the diamond ring, and after getting past being intimidated, I retired the other rings to a box in my dresser drawer, rarely if ever to wear them again.

And now my cherished ring, probably irreplaceable, was gone.

We returned to the medical building. Howard and I glumly walked the halls, checked in the elevator, and went out the door and down the path with our eyes to the ground—except when I looked up to glare at him.

I called our local newspaper to put a reward offer in the

classified section. When I told the woman on the phone the text for the ad, she asked, "Did you *kill* him?" I answered, "Just about!" She wasn't the only one with this reaction. Any woman who heard my tale responded with some variation on *how could he have done such a stupid thing?* Their sisterly solidarity over the foibles of men did make me feel a little better.

I made signs—*Reward: Diamond Wedding Ring*—with my telephone number. I posted them in the medical building by the door and in the elevators, on nearby lampposts, and at the post office, the one place we'd stopped at on the way home. The post-mistress said, "Did you want to strangle him?" and promised she'd keep an eye out, but I had little hope. Rings don't take up much space. Also, if someone had found a diamond wedding band, there was always the possibility of "finders-keepers."

As I accustomed myself to the idea of the permanent loss of my ring, I again began reflecting on its meaning. This time Howard had been the careless one. Was that an indication of how *he* felt about our marriage? He was, of course, very upset, especially as it was his doing, though I knew deep down that I should have taken the ring back as soon as I emerged from the x-ray room. Still, was the ring and all it represented so unimportant to him as to allow him to let it drop off his finger? And why had I not realized sooner that I wasn't wearing it? I was trying to shift my own role so that the guilt could be his alone. I didn't want to take responsibility; I wanted this to be all his fault. I went to bed with a heavy heart.

The telephone rang at seven the following morning. I groggily listened to a woman's voice say, "I think I have your ring."

Instantly awake, I shrieked, "Oh my God, are you sure?"

She described it—"kind of silvery with a lot of stones on it."

I said, starting to cry, "You have my ring. I can't believe it!" She worked in an OB-GYN practice in the building. As she was arriving at work, a Fed Ex man standing on the path outside the building was holding a ring. He told her he had just found it and didn't know what to do with it. The woman had said, "Give it to me. I'll see if someone lost it." Then she'd walked into the building and seen my sign.

I told her I'd be over as soon as I went to the bank. She kindly said the reward wasn't necessary, but I insisted. I withdrew $500.00, a fraction of what the ring was worth, and rushed to the medical building. The office staff, all female, clustered in the reception area and sent for the person who had my ring. She came out smiling and handed me a small envelope with the ring inside. I told them the tale, including that it had been a twenty-fifth anniversary gift, and again got choked up, as did some of the staff. The ring-rescuer and I hugged. Some of the other staff members hugged me as well. I stopped in my hand surgeon's office to tell her, and we hugged, too.

I returned home, all thoughts of marital duress gone.

Howard and I hugged. Other than when receiving good health news, I don't remember ever feeling such relief. I called the lady at the newspaper to cancel the ad. Brimming over with delight, she was almost as excited as I was, as were my sister and friends, all of whom I had called the previous day to moan about my distress, my loss, and its possible *deeper meaning.*

Howard, my ring, and I lived mostly happily ever after for another dozen years, until he died. With the loss of my husband, my rings and his as well were the last things I had on my mind, but as life began to take on its new shape I started thinking about them. What would I do with these rings?

TEN MONTHS AFTER HOWARD'S DEATH, my sister Bunny and I visited Sedona, Arizona, that mystical town in which people seek energy vortices. I don't know or especially care what a vortex is, but I do love the landscape and the dramatic beauty of its red rocks. Bunny and I strolled around a pseudo-historic shopping area—squares surrounded by galleries, jewelry stores, and off-beat or Western clothing emporia.

There was a festival going on with lots of music, kind of "mariachi rock." While Bunny listened to a band, I stepped into a store that sold contemporary jewelry and unusual artwork. Maybe it was the scenery, with its red rocks and infinite horizon, but I was grabbed by a need for a new beginning in the form of a new ring, for me, purchased by me—a statement of me as an individual. I checked the cases. I had a big birthday coming up, and it would be gift from and to me, possibly an opal, my birthstone. As the chunky, mostly silver items in the cases didn't fit my vision, I left. Joining my sister outside the jewelry store, I told her that I'd be looking for a ring to express my individuality as a single person and she kissed me, saying that she thought it was a wonderful idea.

We spotted a few people sipping champagne that the jewelry store was providing, and Bunny decided we should go back in and get some. We entered the store. As she poured us our drinks, over the PA system came Frank Sinatra's voice, singing, of all things, "Fly Me to the Moon"—Howard's and my song. As I had on other mysterious occasions, I wondered whether he was reprimanding or encouraging me. I started to cry, but we agreed that, knowing Howard, it was the latter. And in Sedona, of all places. Sedona, town of mystery. It was just too much.

The ring question remained unresolved until, two months later, I joined my son Edward, daughter-in-law Katie, and grandchildren for Thanksgiving at Katie's parents' home in Pennsylvania. Friday afternoon found me restless and lonely, so Ed and I agreed to go for a ride. To give us a destination I decided to look for earrings for my granddaughter's newly pierced ears. We drove to an antique mall—four large shed-like buildings—arriving just before closing time. We selected one building arbitrarily and wandered in.

I asked the proprietor if she had any earrings. She pointed vaguely down an aisle and said there might be a few there. I meandered over without much hope. Sitting in a glass display case was a pair of tiny gold love-knots with a small amethyst on each. They were perfect. . .but even more perfect, not two inches away from the earrings, was a delicate gold ring with an opal. I called Ed over, sure that the ring would be too small; it fit perfectly, as though it had been designed just for me. As the earrings and ring were being wrapped, my blue mood turned to gold; I was elated. I'm not a mystical person, but once again I wondered about Howard. Had he sent us there, to that particular building on that particular day? To a ring that was exactly what I wanted, that fit me perfectly?

Meanwhile, the fate of my marriage rings remains undetermined. In addition to the wedding bands, I had an elegant engagement ring that I rarely wore except on special occasions that became increasingly infrequent over the years. The engagement ring and diamond band worn together were too flashy, and I couldn't wear the engagement ring on the other hand because an arthritic bump on my right ring finger blocks it.

I've been thinking about a future for the rings. I have two lovely daughters-in-law. Maybe I'll give each of them a ring. Marc's wife is an attorney and, at five-foot-nine is as tall as I once was and can carry such jewelry. She'd probably also like it. Edward's wife, at my current height of five-seven or so, is an artist. I don't know if she's into diamond rings, though she does love the diamond earrings that my son had made from his grandmother's cocktail ring. There are also my grandchildren. Franklin may someday want a lovely engagement ring to give to a special young woman. He might even want to wear his grandfather's wedding ring. And red-headed Nora is going to be a stunner. Who knows, she or her adorable cousin Maya may agree with their grandmother that, as the old song says, diamonds are indeed a girl's best friend.

Wherever my rings end up, I know that I loved and cherished them for all the years I wore them. I've been told that the wedding ring, which in Judaism is supposed to be an unbroken circle, represents the circle of life. I see now that it's true. Rings represent special moments; they make a statement about who we are, whether it's a class ring, a fraternity ring, friendship ring or an opulent diamond wedding band. My own diamond ring was a statement of my husband's love and the twenty-five years we'd spent together. Now its role has changed. Now it's a family heirloom that I hope will find a new role to play among my children and grandchildren. I hope it will represent decades of happy memories for them and their future generations, much as it did for me.

Moving On

I'VE HEARD THAT AN ORDERLY HOUSE leads to an orderly mind. I know that when my brain is scattered and my house cluttered, both contribute to a sense of chaos and confusion. My brain darts around like a hummingbird; I wonder if I should first file papers or pay bills, throw out the junk mail or clean up that huge pile on a nearby table that started life as an ottoman. So many needs exist that I can't alight on one task. I'm paralyzed. I undertake nothing. Sometimes, around midnight, I go on a putting-away and hanging-up binge, getting to bed too late but with some sense of accomplishment.

As I approach two years of living alone, I think more frequently about moving from my house to an apartment. My husband and I had planned to do that as soon as he got through what turned out to be his final surgery and illness. Best laid plans and all that. My greatest fear was realized:

I was left alone in my house, a widow. When Howard was alive, I used to complain to him that we had no empty surfaces. It seemed as though every chair, table, shelf and bureau had something on it, probably because they did. Now, of course, I have no one to blame but myself.

My home is not excessively messy, thanks to the fact that every two weeks I have a cleaning woman, forcing me to clean for the cleaner, as most of us do. Nevertheless, if you live alone and days go by with no one coming to your house, you start to wonder—at least I do—what is the point of clearing the sink of dishes, folding the laundry, or removing the bills to be paid from the couch in the den. There's no one but me to see the clutter. Sometimes my inner self wants things cleaned up and put away, but equally often, I don't really give a damn. I can see how, over time, people living alone find themselves in an awful mess, which finally becomes so overwhelming that deciding where to begin is impossible.

I love my one-story house; it's like a spacious sunny apartment with grass around it. But my garage is reached from the basement and therefore impractical. I can't, for example, carry bundles or suitcases up the stairs. To move myself in the direction of clearing some of the debris from my brain as well as my home, I hired Moving Mavins, a company that will help you get rid of stuff you thought you'd never part with, pack your things and unpack them, and put them away in your new residence. I explained that I wasn't ready to move but wanted to position myself so that, when it was time to take that step, I would not feel engulfed by an overly cluttered house and too many memories.

Moving Mavins arrived—Celia and Grace Ann. Celia was briskly efficient but a little lacking in empathy. Seemingly craving approval, I disposed of one item after the other as they were presented. Although Celia praised my quick decision-making, I felt as though she were figuratively brushing her hands together and moving on to the next item before I'd finished ruminating about the previous one. It was, after all, my life that we were dismantling.

Grace Ann, whose tall, lithe, blue-eyed looks fit her name, seemed more inclined to give me the extra moments that I sometimes needed.

We began with my basement storage room. Although not in view for the casual visitor, it needed to be emptier and neater for a potential buyer. It was also the space that I found most daunting, since it contained the fragments of our past lives, from high school and college yearbooks to discarded furniture. Also lying there were a dozen awards that Howard had insisted upon having laminated that I had no idea what to do with. It also contained his bowling ball and tennis racket, evidence of the accomplished athlete he once had been.

After that first visit, with giant garbage bags the contents of which documented our lives having been removed, Grace Ann returned as a solo act. I never asked why, because I preferred it. Grace Ann turned out to be going through a divorce and move of her own. We did a lot of talking, providing support for one another as we each went through a difficult time. Maybe this was why it took two more visits of three to four hours each to get the storeroom to a manageable state. My son and I made decisions about some of the more difficult sentimental items, like those yearbooks, real estate mementos, and athletic trophies. In the long run we removed most of it, keeping a few with special meaning. I still have drawers full of uncategorized photographs, along with a small wooden plaque with a caricature of my husband and the word "appraiser," given to him by my parents. Now I, too, was playing the role of appraiser, if in a different context. His job had been to determine the monetary value of real property, whereas mine was now concerned with the psychic value of long-held possessions.

Next, we tackled Howard's home office. He had emptied many drawers and shredded their contents after retiring. His enthusiasm for shredding so overtook him that the shredder started to smoke when the sheer volume of papers exceeded its capacity. A melted credit card that gummed up the works finished the job. He'd also found a place for his library of real estate books, to my immense gratitude and relief. Still, reviewing the remaining few appraisals and reading about historic New York City real estate was a slow and painful process, for this was not only about his work; it was about where he had grown up.

Unfolding the floor plan of his parents' apartment in the

famous twin towers of the San Remo—bought by Zero Mostel after Howard's father's death and mother's rapid relocation—unlocked memories of my first visit to exclusive Central Park West as a twenty-year-old from a modest garden apartment in Queens. I could recall my astonishment at a dining room that could seat twenty-four, with a chandelier that displayed, literally, low-hanging fruit—crystal apples, pears, bananas—that made my eyes pop. There was an inlaid brass turtle sitting on the mahogany table that I fooled around with a bit until it emitted a shrill ring and the serving maid walked in, to my mortification. The immense living room could probably have contained my parents' entire apartment. Was that young girl still inside me after a half-century as *Mrs. Guttman,* or had I become, as my daughter-in-law persists in calling me, the family matriarch? Indeed, I felt I was appraising my own life.

We proceeded upstairs. My living room and dining room needed little attention, as I knew which furniture, *chachkas,* and paintings would go when it was time to downsize. The fact that we could leave the kitchen alone was a measure of how little I cook. My office, however, was laden with the detritus of my work history as an educator, concert manager, choir director, and consultant. What to do with the syllabus I created for the class I taught at NYU? What of the brochures I had written during a decade of managing a chamber music series, and the thick loose-leaf books of synagogue choral music? I allowed myself to hold onto those items that would have made me too sad to lose. Someday they would all land in the garbage, but that would be a job for my children.

After nearly fifty years of rheumatoid arthritis, I also had to figure out how far back I needed to keep my health records. I found the surgeon's description of my first knee replacement in 1989, when I was forty-six. Having gotten many years out of each of those titanium-and-plastic prostheses, I was now approaching my fourth replacement.

My den and bedroom Grace Ann and I approached with a much lighter touch, as these are the places where I really live my life. They wouldn't be ready to dismantle until I moved or was carried out.

Now my house looks pristine, in good enough shape to be cleaned up for guests in about ten minutes and for potential purchasers in a day or two. Nevertheless, there remain the embarrassing secret stashes. First, my refrigerator, a receptacle for spoiled food. As my meal preparation is limited to making sandwiches or microwaving, kitchen clutter is limited to junk mail and old receipts covering the table. However, open the fridge, and a mess lurks within, like the month-old container of noodle soup, dried-out cream cheese, spoiled restaurant remains, and an ancient jar of marinara sauce. I'm afraid to open the containers and pour out the contents for fear of horrible odors and mysterious lumps. Should I toss them with their contents intact? Since I can't decide, everything stays until my daughter-in-law Michelle visits. Michelle makes a hobby of throwing away my spoiled food. Some might consider it an intrusion; I consider it a relief, even if she gets a bit overzealous now and then.

Then there's my kitchen junk drawer. I've always thought that everybody must have a junk drawer, and usually it resides in the kitchen. Doesn't everyone need a place to throw unused twist ties, the odd piece of Velcro, candle remains that might be useful in a power outage, superglue, toothpicks that long ago escaped their box, a few tools to help open recalcitrant bottles, tape, and pens and pencils?

On Grace Ann's final visit, she was looking for something to help one of my plants stand upright instead of drooping from the windowsill onto my dish drainer. I saw no escape; I had to open the drawer and take out the aluminum foil, plastic wrap, and large and small baggies that were covering the mess beneath. I cringed. Mumbling that the drawer would need a good cleanup from me, I left the junk on the counter, filled with noble intentions of keeping the drawer exclusively for various food wrappings. I did find new places for the Velcro, glue, and writing implements, but after a day or two, with my cleaning lady's imminent arrival, I sighed and shoved the remaining bits and pieces back in the drawer.

Finally, my bedroom: Grace Ann was looking for a place to put a little makeup pouch. I was ashamed to tell her to open the top drawer of my dresser because I knew what she would find: another mess, the junk drawer of my bedroom. Shamefaced, I muttered that once you got past the top layer it was fairly well organized, which is true. Still, I promised myself that I would reorganize my dresser, and the closet next to it, in the near future.

That was my last session with the lovely and sympathetic Grace Ann, who has carted off so many things, from small pieces of furniture to books that are not dear to me, and who has packed cartons for me to donate to my synagogue bazaar.

I sit in my sun-filled living room and look around. It brings me peace, I think, or does it? The room is in some ways the descendant of my mother-in-law's esthetic: paintings, pedestals, more lamps and clocks than I know what to do with. While Howard was alive, it made sense to live in the middle of all these things that he had brought to the marriage. Now that he's gone, however, I sometimes feel as though I'm living among someone else's possessions. I take stock: the Howard-sized easy chair, the sofa, organ, piano, dining table and chairs, the table my great-grandfather built, the model of the schooner America that I'd bought for Howard's fiftieth birthday, and even an old stereo unit we'd acquired after our marriage. The same for the Chinese rug, a replacement for my mother-in-law's old one that we had been required to keep folded under at one end because, while beautiful, it was too big for our room. (We'd bought the new one a week after her death.) The dining room rug, a smaller one in front of the fireplace, a little rocker, and two small decorative chairs also came from my in-laws, as did a sculpture of a dancing couple in the *shtetl*.

Probably twenty paintings came from Howard's home, but the biggest one, the one you notice the minute you enter, is a Matissean floor-to-ceiling acrylic of a woman walking into a room through French doors. Howard and I bought it together for a long-ago birthday of mine. Our parents hated it, which made us love it all the more.

If Howard and I acquired so many of these things on our own, why do I sometimes feel that I live in somebody else's home? I wonder, does my living room reflect my personality or were we simply adhering to the style set by the items we inherited when my father-in-law died six weeks after our wedding?

When my mother-in-law instantly downsized from eight large rooms to three or four smaller ones, we were the logical repository for her own decluttering process. There we were, newlyweds at twenty-one and twenty-six, with a grand piano, custom-made drapes, an Oriental carpet, paintings, sculpture, and accessories of all types. We never had the opportunity to start with early Salvation Army and graduate to a home built around our taste. Our bedroom started out with a pair of dressers and a bookcase that came from Howard's bedroom; to that we added a French Provincial armoire and night tables that I never liked, sheer custom-made drapes, lamps made from beautiful Chinese vases that we did not select, an intricately carved wood-and-cane headboard that you couldn't lean against, and a custom-made quilted bedspread to complete the ensemble. We acquired these with the help of a decorator who was found for us, as my mother looked on with pride. She had never been able to afford a decorator. I resisted only weakly, for what would I—could I—have said?

Now, all these years later and alone, I wonder if this home is actually a reflection of my preferences—if I've grown into it, or if I've just resigned myself to living with it. The two paintings that I truly adored, and wanted from my mother-in-law's home when she died, went to my sister-in-law. One of them she immediately sold for a great deal of money. I never saw it again.

I wonder if I'll have to reevaluate—appraise—all the items in my home and decide if they are indeed my taste or a reflection and adaptation of somebody else's. Then again, these are the heritage of my husband and meaningful to my children. For the time being, I'll probably continue to live with them. I could do worse.

Strangely, as I get rid of extraneous and obsolete parts of my life, I become increasingly comfortable with the idea of staying in my home. So here I am, in a mostly decluttered house, still craving a doorman and fewer bills to pay and no landscaper to deal with but attracted by the idea of remaining here with my memories. Perhaps if I ever have a new man in my life, I'll want to embark on moving ahead to a new adventure. Not right now, though, for I'm comfortable here. My non-mess and I will remain until further notice.

Three Years, Going on Four: The Upside

A NEVER-MARRIED FRIEND IN HIS FIFTIES once said to me, "There's something to be said for living alone." I agree, but I wonder if any widows or widowers—that is, those who profess to have dearly loved their late spouses—ever acknowledge that there is indeed an upside. And am I the only one who feels this way, or the only one who admits it?

Some months after Howard died I attended a dinner party and began a conversation with a woman who'd been widowed about three years earlier. At some point I confessed that there were certain things I liked about living alone and being accountable to no one but myself. She told me I was very brave to say that and seemed delighted to hear it, as though I had given her permission to feel the same way. Perhaps this is a forbidden topic; even after two years, I'm not sure of the protocol. Whether or not we are "allowed" to enjoy anything about being alone, I've found several positives, listed here in the order in which they floated to the surface of my brain. Other than number one, I can't find any significance in the order. Some are important, others trivial, but on the off-chance that some higher force provided this order for me, I am leaving it as is. Undoubtedly, you could think of more.

I like not having to worry about anybody's needs but my own. Perhaps if there were a new love in my life, I'd be concerned about him, but right now I can be completely self-centered, and maybe I deserve to be, as recompense for coping with the loss of my husband. I like sleeping on my own schedule, going to bed when I wish, and staying there until I want to get up. I like eating whenever I want to, even having a snack in bed at 2:00 a.m. I may not do it very often, but I like knowing that I can.

I make my own eating decisions, again without taking anyone else into consideration. I can have a peanut butter sandwich for dinner. Howard was never demanding about food, which was fortunate as I don't enjoy cooking. But the gender roles persisted to the extent that, eight to ten times a year, he would come home with dinner for us, immensely pleased that he had thought to do it; the rest of the time, it was usually my responsibility to decide on and provide the meal, whether cooked or ordered. My mother called me a lazy eater, as I would take the food that was closest at hand and required the least preparation. She was right, as my current eating habits indicate.

Despite the sometimes oppressive silence of an empty house, I do also love the absence of the constant barrage of baseball, football, and basketball, especially as the seasons extended over the year, running into one another and never giving me a few weeks' respite. I don't have to shut my ears to the histrionics of the announcer or the muted screaming of fans in the stadium. Nor do I have to wince at my normally even-tempered husband's response to it—his continuous, if knowledgeable, commentary that made me wish he had become a professional sports announcer, his yelling, whooping with joy when the (Yankees, Giants, Knicks, Nets) did well and cursing almost violently when they didn't. I don't miss that at all—except now and then. And I still laugh when I remember Howard's hilariously pitch-perfect imitation of a golf announcer whispering into the microphone so as not to disturb the player at the tee.

Conversely, I can watch programs that he would tease me about, that I would quickly turn off if he was in the vicinity: *Friends*. *Big Bang Theory*. Even the truly guilty pleasure of *Say Yes to the Dress*, which I would never have viewed with Howard nearby. (What can I say? I love brides.)

I spend money as I wish. Howard was very generous, but I feel a new, grown-up freedom in managing my own funds. Indeed, it *is* my money. It used to be ours, and most of it came from his family. Now it's mine, and for the first time I am "independently wealthy." Well, not wealthy by today's standards, but most definitely comfortable. Even my friend Stef, who, eighteen years after her husband's death, still will not go to the cemetery alone because of the anguish it causes her, even *she* had a deck added to her house shortly after her husband died. He'd been too worried about being broke in old age ever to spend an extra dime other than on traveling, which was his passion. Sadly, he didn't make it to old age, so the point was lost.

There's no one to say, "You're still on the phone?" when I stay up late talking to Stef. I still picture Howard in his big green fleece robe, with the cane and later the walker, coming to the den doorway and gently chiding me for not hanging up and coming to bed. Sometimes I listened and quickly ended the call; other times I just glared and continued talking. I like that no one is monitoring me, though when it's midnight and I'm still on the phone, in my mind that green bathrobe is always nearby.

Moving into the bedroom, the same queen-sized bed that had become too small for us, that I had planned to replace with a king, that had a restless Howard kicking me during the night and scratching me with his toenails, is now one of my happier places. There's no denying that I would love to share the bed on occasion, but meanwhile, for the first time in my life, I sprawl to my heart's content. I turn off the light with the TV remote and a book nearby, with my iPhone next to the pillow so I'm lulled to sleep by an audiobook, favorite music or even Tibetan singing bowls. If my home is my castle, my bed is its keep, my inner sanctum.

I can leave all my cosmetics on the bathroom sink. As the vanity is relatively small, when Howard was alive, after using them I'd have to put away any hair product, moisturizer, or foundation, to say nothing of lipstick and hairbrush. Now they stay on the sink unless the cleaning lady is coming, at which point I stash them all in the cabinet and drawer. True luxury. And I can use both sides of the sink. It took me a little while to realize that I could do this. After Howard died I automatically put everything away each morning, until one day reality dawned—why was I doing it? I felt a strange combination of melancholy and exhilaration.

More sink issues: My husband was easygoing almost to a fault, but he truly hated seeing my hair in the sink, and it was inescapably there, especially when I was on a medication that caused temporary hair loss. As he had so few dislikes, I accommodated him by carefully wiping out any strands and throwing them in the wastebasket so as not to clog the drain. Now I let it collect before I do that. I even let some go down the drain, feeling sinful as it swirls around and disappears.

Speaking of sinks, there's the matter of dirty dishes. Among my friends, some postponed cleaning up after dinner, and others didn't leave the kitchen until the sink was clean and the dishwasher loaded. In our family it was not an issue, as Howard took possession of the dishwasher almost from the time we were married. Initially I carried out his mission of rinsing, loading, unloading, and shelving.

Now, however, with no one to see, I admit to sometimes allowing dirty dishes to pile up and even (gracious me!) using clean dishes and silverware straight from the dishwasher instead of putting them away in their cabinets. So do some friends of mine. The point is that, even if we don't want to leave the dishes, *we know we can.*

For the first time in my sister's and my adult lives, we get to spend more time together, since she's been single for many years and I'm no longer drawn home to Howard. Part of me dearly wishes that he was waiting for me, but I have to acknowledge that it's a weight off my shoulders that only I decide when it's time to go home. I don't know that I'd ever had that experience before Howard's death. I was away at college for four years, but we had a curfew. (The boys did not.) Then I lived away from my parents for one year before getting married, but it was in the home of a widow who prepared dinner for us, us being me and another teacher who lived there as well. We were, in a sense, accountable to our landlady.

I can "double dip." If I'm alone and biting a piece of celery, potato chip, or cracker, and I want some additional dip, I can just take it. I suppose some would say that double dipping is allowable with your spouse or partner, but to me it was like sharing a toothbrush—a touch yucky. Certainly, if you're kissing you are already sharing mouth germs, but I don't know. . .I was never comfortable with double dipping even with Howard. But alone? I can dip away.

Howard and I traveled in both the United States and

abroad. We had a wonderful time, even when it became difficult for him. Howard wanted to see Australia; we both did. Now I may never go there because I can't imagine seeing it without him. But I can travel to places that never interested him, like China. I may never get to China but *I can do it if I want to.*

I don't have to nag Howard either. That may sound crazy. Why would I have *had* to nag him? Because I was trying to get him to take care of himself and stay alive. I'm utterly convinced that that's the reason we see so many older couples in which the wife is a perpetual nag. Sadly, Howard did not stay alive, so no more nagging is necessary. And contrary to appearances, I hated being a nag.

And finally, I've had new, liberating adventures. I've made new friends. I've written a book. I've had serendipitous experiences that never would have happened had I been half a couple. If I've met a variety of men of varying degrees of strangeness, it has broadened my knowledge of human nature. I've met some women with whom I've felt an almost instant rapport, almost making me wish they were men. One woman I met on the bus from Framingham, Massachusetts, to New York City turned out to be a writer and writing professor; by the time we disembarked she'd explained to me how to find a literary agent and, as she gave me her card, wished me all kinds of good luck. I've gotten serious about my writing, after twenty or thirty years of dabbling. I've taken writing classes and workshops and now count a whole new circle of both riders and writers.

Aldous Huxley said, "My fate cannot be mastered; it can only be collaborated with and thereby, to some extent, directed. Nor am I the captain of my soul; I am only its noisiest passenger." To some extent, and for the first time in my life, I feel as though I'm indeed the master of my fate, unless and until illness or age overtakes me. It took me awhile, but here I am. I'd rather Howard be here with me, with both his strengths and his foibles, but there's also an upside to being alone if only we look for it and let ourselves acknowledge it.

My friend Stef says that, however many upsides there are, they don't compensate for the loss of her husband. I admit she has a point, but we accomplish little by dwelling on what we cannot fix. We can either bemoan the fact of our loneliness—and I guess all of us do at times—or consider its advantages, which really do exist. Even our best friends at some point will begin to suffer from compassion fatigue. They don't want to hear us moan, if for no other reason than that it reminds them of their own mortality or potential loneliness. Our state of mind reflects the old saying about the glass being half empty or half full. Maybe it's not half full; maybe it is one-third full. But I suggest that it's the fact rather than the degree of fullness that's important.

As I become increasingly confident, maybe that glass will eventually fill up completely. Maybe not. Anything is possible.

Bugs Black Blood

MY FATHER HAD A WONDERFUL sense of humor. He loved to tell jokes, and he loved to fool around with us by reciting tongue twisters he'd learned from his own father that we'd struggle to repeat, finally and proudly mastering them. Some were long and complex, like, "She sells seashells by the seashore," or "United States twin screw steel cruisers." He of course was delighted when we inevitably said, "screws her" instead of "cruisers." Others were short and sweet but had to be repeated three times, like, "Toy boat toy boat toy boat," or "Bugs black blood bugs black blood bugs black blood." (For the record, my dictation software can't do it either.)

I was thinking about that last one recently as I stepped on a pair of large insects that had invaded my bathroom about a week apart, each time when the weather had gotten unexpectedly and briefly warm. They were totally different species, the first one being beetle-like and the second looking like a wasp that didn't know how to fly. For the most part, I've never been squeamish about killing bugs, other than the ones that you just know are going to crunch when you step on them. I simply cannot tolerate the crunch. Fortunately, I've rarely encountered them, and when I have, there have been other people around. If I ever have to deal with a crunch bug on my own, I guess I'll find out what I'm truly made of.

My friend Stef is a great humanitarian, or perhaps bugatarian. She can't stand the idea of killing things. She'd rather place a cup over the offending creature, slide a piece of paper between the cup and the wall, and then release the insect somewhere outdoors. She did this with mice also, as she thought they were cute and sweet—until a herd of mice invaded her pantry. (Apparently a mouse group is sometimes called a "mischief." Peculiar but fitting. The most common term is apparently "nest," but that's far less disturbing, evoking as it does baby birds.) No matter what kind of humane trap she set, they wouldn't go away. When she saw one flatten itself and slide under the door of the pantry into her kitchen, dismay, or perhaps horror, outweighed humanitarianism and she called the exterminator.

But for me, killing was never the big problem; disposal—that's the issue. Flies, mosquitoes, spiders, I take a tissue or paper towel, pick them up, throw them away. My husband had a great technique for catching and killing flying insects. He turned off all the lights and turned on the television set. Without fail, the insects were drawn to the TV screen, and as they crawled around, my hero smacked them with a magazine. As he wiped off the screen and threw away the remains, I was as impressed as if he had been a Samurai warrior. He was a good teacher, and I've done it myself once or twice.

But those big ones that crawl around on the wall or the floor (I'm not afraid to give them a flick so they fall off the wall), the ones you can feel inside the tissue, I admit it, I can't bring myself to pick them up and toss them.

And so it was that a dead bug, black blood and all, reposed in my bathroom for several days. I had been lucky with its predecessor, because my son and his family happened to visit, arriving just a day or so after I'd killed that one. As my son headed for the bathroom, I casually said, "And while you're in there, would you please get rid of the dead bug on the floor." But for this latter one, I wasn't expecting any visitors, and my biweekly cleaning lady had been there just a day or two earlier. Each day, when I brushed my teeth, showered or made other use of the bathroom, there it was, looking at me. Actually, it was facing away from me so I guess I was looking at it. Had it magically disappeared, I think that would've been worse, because then I would have had to speculate about the creature that had removed it. I had vague hopes that the body would dry out and become desiccated and, if not disappear, flatten out so that I could pick it up. It didn't happen.

The insect was on the floor near one wall, lying beneath my big gold bath towel that hangs on a hook, sometimes drooping perilously near the floor. Occasionally it falls down, which would have meant falling on top of the bug. I couldn't stand the thought of that, so I was careful to grab a good handful of terrycloth when I hung the towel on its hook.

In the three years since my husband died, I've given a lot of thought to my developing independence. Like it or not, I do handle most things on my own, with occasional assistance from a friend or my kids. I was not about to call my son, who lives twenty minutes away, and ask him to please make time to come over and dispose of a dead insect. A male friend who would have done it was traveling, and anyway, the role of helpless female doesn't suit me very well. It never has. And as for my women friends, dammit, if they could do it, I could too.

Eventually, the obvious solution occurred to me. I don't know why I hadn't thought of it sooner. As I sat in the bathroom eyeing the inert insect body, flightless wings still intact, I realized that all I had to do was bring in my little handheld vacuum cleaner and, as they say, suck it up. Once I knew what I'd do, I kept forgetting to bring it from the kitchen to the bathroom. I'd remember in the bathroom and forget in the kitchen. This went on for another day or two, until the moment when I said to myself, "This is ridiculous." I went to the kitchen, grabbed the little vacuum, marched right back into the bathroom before I could forget, and got rid of the damn thing.

So much for bugs black blood. Another small triumph in the life of a single older woman.

The Neat Side of the Bed

I AWAKEN, THROW OFF THE COVERS, roll out of bed and head for the bathroom. Maybe I step right into the shower and get dressed, or not. Maybe I meditate or just go back to sleep. Whatever the routine, at some point I glance at my bed, where I see that one side—my side—is in disarray, reflecting what kind of night it's been, and the other side, almost always, has remained pristine. (No, officer, the bed has not been slept in, or rather, half of it has not.) That was his side—my husband's—and he is gone. Dead, that is.

I remember, shortly before our wedding, when Howard and I bought our first bed, a queen size. A so-called "technical virgin," I remember the excitement I felt as we lay down first on one bed and then another, seeing which suited both of us best, as if it mattered. I just wanted that big bed that would be waiting for us after our honeymoon. I had never shared a bed with a man before, or a woman either. It was so exciting—our bed! I can still see the apartment building from the George Washington Bridge, and when I glance at it as I drive across, that thrill of knowing that our home was awaiting us still runs through my body, fifty-six years later.

Neither of us ever staked out one side of the bed for our exclusive use. Generally, I got the side near the bathroom. In our New Jersey home, it was on the left; the summer house had it on the right. In the last year or two of Howard's life, he increasingly needed a walker to stay on his feet. At that point, I ceded the bathroom side to him.

At three years without him, I find myself contemplating that neat half. What is it good for? Why do I have it? What should I do with it? I can't get rid of it unless I buy a new bed, and I don't want to sleep in a twin after decades of sprawling in a queen- or king-size bed.

One way I put it to use is by keeping the heating pad on that side. If my back is aching, I need only lie down on it and let the warmth of the pad soothe me. When Howard was here, he would rub my back if it ached, a far better solution than even the best heating pad, but we take what we can get. I also use the far side of the bed to hide things, like the footstool I need to help me zip and unzip boots, or the humidifier that feebly fights against my dry eyes and nose.

I've learned that, when my husband accused me of being a blanket hog, he was not always wrong. There are mornings when my blanket is diagonal, the result of my tugging at it during a restless night. Of course, I accused him equally vociferously. I wish I could wake him up to tell him that we were equal-opportunity blanket hogs. What better way to test that than by having one person sleep in a bed built for two?

At our summer home we slept in a king-size bed. It had come with the house, and when we replaced it we automatically bought the same size. It's utterly ridiculous, to say nothing of lonely, to be sleeping there solo, but I'm not ready to throw out a perfectly good bed and buy a smaller one. Also, I had harbored a hope that eventually that side would be occupied by another soul, preferably long of leg and broad of shoulder. As time goes by, that possibility is diminishing. It seems to me that by the time somebody else came along, a distinctly unlikely prospect, he would be too tired or too old to make the seventy-mile drive to the lake—or the three-foot hike across the bed, come to think of it.

The neat side of the bed stares back at me almost reproachfully. It's not fulfilling its function; it's being neglected. That's not entirely true, as I often sleep in the shape of a "C," with my own long legs resting on the sheet as they used to rest on my husband's shins. (As Howard lay unconscious in hospice, I sat on a chair next to him, leg snuggled up to his on the bed, just as we always had done.)

If I were into stuffed animals, I could pile a bunch on that side, grabbing some fake fur if I was really desperate to cuddle with something. Better still, though worse for me, I could get a pet and let it join me in bed. The only problem is that I find it nauseating to think of an animal that has walked God knows where lying in my bed. Human animals are much more my thing.

I guess I could sleep in the middle, but then if I wanted to get out of bed quickly to run to the bathroom, I would first have to shimmy over to one side, a bit of a chore when you are half asleep and arthritic. I have a daughter-in-law who sleeps with a body pillow, a cylinder-shaped thing about three feet long that seemingly is meant as a cuddle crutch. I think it makes her back feel better. I have to look into that, but I'm sure I'd prefer a body to a pillow.

In the course of a conversation with one my friends recently, I learned that some children even as young as seven or eight now have their own double beds. I was stunned, perhaps because in childhood and through high school I slept on what was called a "youth bed" and at other times on a studio couch, a narrow bed that could open up to accommodate another skinny person. My first encounter with a twin bed was at college. It seemed luxuriously large. What will these kids, trained from childhood to occupy an entire large bed, do when they encounter a situation that requires sharing? I guess they can share the bed to satisfy sexual desires and then go their separate ways to sleep. My friend Stef's husband did that, because he couldn't tolerate her snoring. It didn't seem to hamper their relationship, so perhaps there's something in it.

As for me, much as I like being able to sprawl when the spirit moves me, I would prefer to return to the days of yesteryear, when my mate and I snuggled on a cold night, lay quietly together talking, in shared intimacy along with the shared bed. It might even be worth the occasional leg kick, possibly even the four-inch scratch on my instep from his toenail.

I know I'm not alone in trying to solve this dilemma, as now and then I hear from others in the same position. One woman sleeps with her husband's pajamas lying next to her. I was so touched when she told me, but I can't help envisioning this flat pair of PJs that once had been three-dimensional. There's something tragic about it. Howard's build was almost bulky, so that when he pulled me on top of him I felt as though I were lying on a platform. The two-dimensional emptiness of unoccupied pajamas, to me, only underscores the loss of their former occupant.

Early in our marriage, I had gradually worked my husband out of his PJs and into underwear or even less for sleeping. He still owned pajamas, but mostly they stayed in the drawer unless it was an extremely cold night or, maybe, if we were going to have house guests. You never know what the middle of the night can bring. For example, our friends Joe and Nancy were sleeping happily at our lake house when, in the darkest night, the heavens opened up. The skylight in their room was open, just above their bed, so at 2:00 AM, there we were knocking on their door with a long rod used for closing the skylight. Joe, ever alert, grabbed it and, in a few seconds, had taken care of the problem. Now that I think of it, I'm pretty sure Howard was in his underwear for this little escapade. Joe, too.

I guess I could have grabbed some of Howard's underwear to snuggle with, but for the fact that my kids got a little overzealous in helping me get rid of clothing after he died. I appreciated their assistance more than I can say, but when I ache with arthritis, I remember how his always-warm undershirts soothed my body. I would have kept a few for myself.

I had another friend, older, now also gone, who was presented with an American flag at her husband's funeral. He had been in military intelligence during World War II and was very proud of that. At the funeral there was a recorded trumpet playing taps, and a six-gun salute. As is the custom, she was given a large flag folded into the traditional triangle. She told me once that she slept with that tightly packed flag next to her, that it made her feel her husband's presence. At least it had some bulk, unlike pajamas.

With the passage of time the dilemma has tilted slightly. Formerly it was a question of how to use the empty side temporarily until it might again be occupied; as that possibility fades, it's about redefining my relationship with this sixty-by-eighty-inch piece of real estate that belongs to me alone.

Out of consideration for my husband, I didn't snack in bed, nor did he. Now I sometimes do, so I try to be careful not to get crumbs in the bed. The thing is, if I do, I can just switch sides for a comfortable night's sleep. I can put the television on at any hour of the day or night, and not worry about the sound or the flickering screen bothering him. I can meditate without fear of interruption. That's not about size so much as privacy. Here's one: on those nights of restless, perspiration-filled sleep, all I need do to refresh myself is switch sides. Or I can throw off the blanket altogether until I'm ready to be covered again, and not have it fall on the floor.

And, finally, I can release my inner slob. I've been known to go to sleep surrounded by my tech toys: cell phone, landline, TV remote, now and then my laptop, plus maybe a book. Only a solo sleeper in a big bed can accommodate that.

But who am I kidding? I like having all the space to spread out, but I do wish that, once in a while, someone else were there with whom I could share it. So when the time comes to replace this bed, it'll probably be with another queen size. You never know where life takes you and, like the good Girl Scout I was, my motto is Be Prepared.

My Coffee with Amir

WHEN CONSIDERING MY DATING EXPERIENCES, I certainly wouldn't call them exotic—or erotic—except perhaps for my coffee date with Amir.

I have a bi-weekly massage therapist who comes to my house, one of my great indulgences in the effort to keep my body moving. Much as with barbers and hairdressers, there's something about having someone's hands on you that invites confidences, so Melissa was well aware of the fact that I craved someone's hands on my body besides hers. One day she asked if I might be interested in meeting an eighty-four-year-old gentleman who was very lonely, having lost his wife a couple of years before. She didn't know him personally, but he was a friend of the deceased father of an ophthalmologist she'd been dating. He was Persian and named Amir.

At the very least, this had the potential to be interesting. I of course said, why not? My Match.com attempts had not been especially inspiring, ranging as they had from tolerable to terrible.

I told her that I had houseguests for a few days and asked that he please wait until after the following Monday— like Tuesday, for example. But late Monday afternoon he called and, though my guests were gone, I let it go to voicemail. I wasn't ready, and he seemed a little too eager. I waited until the following evening to call him back.

Persian of course meant Iranian, which meant, most likely, Muslim, from a country that wants to destroy Israel. I'm not a rabid Zionist, but the existence of Israel, whether I approve of all its actions or not, is very important to me. I had asked Melissa if this man knew that I was Jewish. She was a little vague but said she thought he did. I've never had a need to limit my social life to Jews, but I did wonder how a person from Iran would perceive me.

Amir spoke very hastily on the telephone. He seemed somewhat nervous, almost business-like, but if anything, that was a bit endearing. We made an appointment to meet for coffee at a Starbucks located between our two New Jersey towns. I asked him what he looked like, and he brushed that off, saying, "I'm eighty-four years old, and I am not handsome, so what difference does it make?" I told him that I was on the tall side with dark, curly hair, and we left it at that.

Melissa is Filipina and Catholic. The ophthalmologist,

with whom she hoped to establish a relationship, was also Persian and Muslim. And here I was, a Jew. Only in America. Part of her motivation for playing matchmaker was that it gave her more opportunities to connect with the eye doctor. She, too, was sick of Match.com.

As our appointment date loomed, I became somewhat trepidatious, upset that my hair had decided to be frizzy instead of curly, and unable to figure out what to wear. For previous such assignations, I had put together a go to outfit of black jeans, various tops, boots, and a jacket. But an extra seven pounds had made the jeans uncomfortably snug, which is to say that I couldn't zip them, so I was back to square one. Something told me that, since he was neither young nor American-born, I shouldn't be too casual.

The morning of our appointment, the massage therapist visited me, and while under her skilled hands I finally decided what to wear: a nice pair of slacks, boots, an elegant scarf, and a sweater. It was one of those semi-nasty spring days, too warm for a jacket and too cool for lightweight clothes. I jumped into the shower and dampened my hair, following that with "product" that I hoped would calm it down and turn it back into curls, more or less. I laughed at myself, recalling going through this same nonsense before a blind date at college decades before. The mating game remains the same. With people living longer, I can imagine the ninety-five-to-one hundred-year-olds, still concerned about how they look, trying to stand tall behind their walkers or not appear too dependent on their canes. Having spent my share of time on walkers and canes post-knee-replacement, I'm not without empathy. And how can we ever belittle the impulse to be attractive at any age?

I wasn't exactly certain of the Starbucks location and my GPS insisted that it was in a completely different neighborhood from where Amir had described it. Using half GPS and half brain, off I went, allowing plenty of time in case I was mistaken. I arrived fifteen minutes early and pulled in to one of the few parking spaces, almost in front of Starbucks. Standing outside, smoking a cigarette, was an older man wearing a suit and tie, Burberry scarf thrown around his neck with studied casualness, a look I had never seen on an American man. He, too, wanted to look his best, though the air of sophistication was marred somewhat by the trouser leg that was stuck in his sock. Clearly, he needed a woman to tell him to fix this on the way out the door. My instinct about my own wardrobe had been correct, I was relieved to note.

He had a full head of wavy white hair and was, in fact, rather good-looking in a weathered kind of way. He was a bit taller than I am, maybe five foot nine, with a wiry build and a strong-featured tanned face bearing the scars of youthful acne. He looked somehow worldly, or maybe world-weary. He definitely seemed to be watching for someone, pacing back and forth and looking up and down the lot.

I exited my car, timing it so that I could sneak behind him into Starbucks. There was nobody in there over the age of forty, so I was pretty sure that Amir was the man I had been spying on. Eventually he turned, saw me through the window, and came in. We introduced ourselves and shook hands. Having nothing to lose, I told him that I had seen him but had not been sure it was he because he'd said he wasn't handsome. I couldn't believe it; the second sentence out of my mouth was a flirtatious comment. When had I turned into this Jezebel? However, it was apparently the right thing to say, because he looked very pleased.

Taking my elbow, Amir escorted me to the counter and told me that I should order and then find us seats while he brought the drinks. It was a very polite take-charge move that I appreciated. It eliminated the issue of whether I was paying for myself or not, unlike the creep who'd greeted me at a coffee shop with, "You buy the coffee over there."

The only place I could find to sit was at a counter along the window, so we hopped, or climbed, onto a couple of barstools with our drinks. When he brought over my iced coffee, I'd said I was just going to get a straw, and he had insisted that he would and brought back two, of different diameters, so I could take my choice. A sweet gesture, I thought.

I'd ordered iced coffee as a strategy to minimize the limitations of my arthritic and shaky hands. I didn't have to pick it up; I could just lean over and sip from the straw. I thought I was very clever, until he took out a pen and small notepad and explained that he had mislaid my telephone number and would I please write it down for him. The jig was up; I slowly and carefully wrote my long name, followed by my phone number. As he watched, he gently said, "I have that problem also with my hand shaking. Sometimes I can't write at all, and other times it's fine." There was such kindness in his voice. At that moment, I admit it: I melted.

The conversation was far-ranging. He said he'd had a sad life. I learned about his two sons who had both died young—one at the wheel of a truck and the other of a heart attack—and his granddaughter, who lives in Los Angeles. He showed me photographs of the sons, who had been extraordinarily handsome, as well as a recent photo of him and his late wife (plump attractive blonde), and another of the two of them, undoubtedly taken shortly after they were married. They were a slim, dark-haired, serious-faced young couple. I was internally mortified by my own prejudices; I wondered what his politics were and those of his sons. I gathered that, when the Shah was driven out of office, it had been time for them to leave the country. It was obvious how lonely he was and how he craved company. His innate sophistication and intelligence were obvious as well.

Amir told me what kind of wine he drinks (Muslim or not), what kind of food he likes to eat and at which restaurants, where his apartment was, what kind of work he'd done as a lawyer and judge in Iran, and he asked me similar questions. He told me that, for thirty-five years, he'd traveled back and forth between Iran and the United States. I wondered why. Struck by how old-world he seemed, I fell back into my standard behavioral pattern that I use in times of discomfort, that is, I tried to warn him off. I told him that I was "very American," as two grandparents had come here in the 1890s and one grandfather had been born here and one grandmother in Scotland, brought here at the age of two. Then I asked him if he knew I was Jewish and found out that indeed, he did not. He brushed that off by saying that most of the neighbors in his building were also Jewish. Then he started quoting to me from the Torah, as he reads books from many religions. It was fascinating, as he had found in the Torah all kinds of stories of evil and perversion—not the kind of stuff you learn in religious school. I checked them out later and they were all true, which was disconcerting. I was sure I could find similar examples in the Quran, if it came to that.

He was a toucher, leaning forward to touch my arm or even my leg to emphasize something he was saying. I really didn't mind, as I felt that was part of his culture. Also, it didn't seem lascivious, perhaps because of his age. He stated that he liked me because I was "smart and well-educated." He also said he liked my honesty because "everybody lies."

About an hour into our conversation, he said he wanted to ask me a personal question. I shrugged and said that was fine, as I've found that these fix-ups and online dates can become very frank very quickly. We say things that we never would have said when we were young, at least not so soon. It's as though we know that time is short, and we can't waste any of that precious time on preliminaries. He said it was about sex. ". . .I mean, do you like sex?"

I burst out laughing. I had no idea how to react. He quickly added that, in his country, he would never ask a woman such a question, but that here people seem much more open about it. I told him that I love sex, but I don't know whether that was a turn-on or the opposite. After all, at eighty-four—which I later found out was really eighty-six, speaking of lies—maybe he would prefer a woman who was *not* interested in that sort of thing.

He did talk a great deal about going out to dinner every week and about wanting me to see his apartment. Yikes. I responded that I might love sex but I was not about to jump into bed with him. He quickly agreed and said of course not. I still have no idea what to make of that. As I was talking about not jumping into bed with him, part of me was observing it from a distance, marveling at the scenario and conversation between a woman in her middle seventies and a man in his middle eighties who had met only an hour earlier. I guess we're not dead until we're dead. I wondered what the millennials scattered around the room, typing on their laptops, would have thought had they heard us.

Our coffees long since finished, it seemed that it would be obnoxious to stay at Starbucks any longer. He gave me his card and escorted me to my car, telling me that he would be away over the weekend but would call me on Monday. He followed that with a quick kiss on either side of my face,

Parisian style. I wasn't sure how I felt about seeing him again but decided to reserve judgment. As I was backing my car out of the parking space, he was standing in front flapping his hand up and down. It seemed like an odd goodbye until I realized that he was directing my driving. Once again, a take-charge kind of guy. I gave a wave and drove away.

On the way home, with no preamble, I burst into tears. I did something I hadn't done in a long time, yelling at my dead husband for leaving me alone to have to deal with all this stuff. Much as Howard and I bickered, much as caregiving for one another exhausted us, much as I sometimes longed for peace and quiet with no one to bother me, our relationship had evolved into one of loving comfort and security. Despite all that we had been through together, or maybe because of it, we both felt very fortunate. I didn't want to be going through all this dating stuff again, and I could suddenly understand why so many women don't bother to make the effort. I thought that it would be hard enough to get together with a nice Jewish boy from the Bronx, but to develop any kind of relationship with an eighty-four-year-old man from Iran, whose views on many subjects were evidently very different from my own, might be more than I could handle.

I didn't know what I would say when he called on Monday. I agonized. I didn't know if I wanted to see him again, as I didn't want to give him any ideas about a developing sexual relationship. I would love to once again see and have access to a man's body, even an old one, but not this one. Then I thought that perhaps I could make that clear and enjoy having dinners and learning about a new culture. It's always a healthy thing to broaden one's perspective, I told myself. And here was someone who was not put off by my messed-up hands, a real bonus.

I vacillated for three days, trying to figure out how to handle it. I thought that maybe I wouldn't take it further, despite the fact that the time I'd spent with him was a hell of a lot more interesting than with most of the guys I'd met so far. In fact, he was not a *guy*, he was a *man*. That was very much in his favor. I eventually concluded that I would see what he had to say and probably have dinner with him. This was one of the very rare times that a man had made it clear that he wanted to see me again. Okay, I thought, I'm game. I'll give it a shot.

Monday arrived. Monday passed. Amir never called me. He has not, to this day. Go figure.

Three Reunions

A STORY FOR THESE TIMES. On a Friday evening in June 2019 I entered the old Gothic-style building followed by my friend Joan, her aged but agile husband behind her. The disembodied voice of a student greeter said to me, "'69?"

Taken aback, I stammered, "No—uh, '59."

The voice said, "Wow." A good start to a high school reunion, I thought. After checking in and getting our badges with our sixty-year-old yearbook pictures on them, Joan and I looked around in some confusion, not sure where to go next.

A group of laughing people emerged from the auditorium, and I heard a pleasant male voice call out my name. I turned and looked at the group, in particular at one very tall man, the one whose voice I'd heard. He seemed familiar. I admit I glanced at his name tag. "Richard!" I yelled, as we embraced. At that moment, my brain suddenly reminded me, "Hey, kiddo, he's a widower." His wife had met an untimely death years earlier.

There was another man nearby, recently widowed and still handsome, but it was Richard I really wanted to talk to. I knew him somewhat because I'd had some involvement in earlier reunions, as had he and his wife. I'd also managed a concert series on which she had performed. She'd been a wonderful woman, brilliant, talented and kind, and I'd been very sad at the news of her death. Now, with my husband gone as well, my reaction was different—dare I say happy? Curious, at any rate. To be honest, I hadn't expected to still be alone two and a half years later. Don't ask me why, but I thought I would be with someone. Someone had other ideas.

We were shunted to the basement, our former cafeteria, and offered less than tempting hors d'oeuvres, but the food wasn't the point; we were just glad to see each other. All around us, people were shrieking and hugging and snapping photos. Considering that we were the oldest graduating class aside from those who were lumped into "Class of '58 and before," we didn't look too bad. Many of us were reasonably recognizable under gray or bald heads and behind our wrinkles, but then we were the ones who were there, about ten percent of our original graduating class of 507.

I squeezed my way to one of the round tables and sat down on a remarkably uncomfortable stool that was bolted to it. I listened to Richard and two other guys who were still his close friends. We talked as well, falling quickly into an easy rhythm. He told me he wasn't coming to the day-long festivities on Saturday because he hated the new high school building. I was surprised by his reaction. Yes, the building lacked the charm and mystery of its predecessor, but was that enough to make you miss seeing old classmates?

Sunday would round out the weekend with a fundraising brunch at somebody's apartment. He asked if I was going to be there. I told him I hadn't decided and he said, "Oh, come! I'm going."

You bet I will, I immediately thought.

As soon as I arrived home that evening I emailed our class alumni director, who was close to Richard. I asked her if there was a woman in his life. She didn't give me a direct answer, saying that he spends a lot of time with his grandchildren and encouraging me to come to the brunch. I realized later that he could have had ten women, and she still would have urged me to come. She wanted to raise money.

I arrived a little late to find about twenty-five people sitting in a circle, looking rather like a support group for nicely dressed, maybe slightly bohemian, senior citizens. There was one empty seat, next to Richard. I made a dive for it. "You made it!" he said.

Smiling, I twinkled back, "I did—" I, who have never been much of a twinkler.

For the next couple of hours we spent a lot of time

catching up, laughing, and talking more easily than I had with any man since Howard's death. I couldn't believe how comfortable I was. No self-consciousness about my arthritic and trembling hands. It didn't seem to matter—finally.

When it was time to leave, I did something I'd never done before; I told Richard that I had so enjoyed spending time with him, and that I'd love to see more of him. I gave him my business card. With a big smile, he took it and said, "I will put it right in my wallet," which he did, on the spot. I floated out of the apartment but apparently, the card did not float out of the wallet. I heard nothing from him.

About a month later I received my opera subscription tickets. Since I knew he was a fan and I had nothing to lose, I used that as a pretext for getting in touch. I sent an email, reiterating how much I had enjoyed seeing him at the reunion and asking if he'd like to join me at one or two operas. I heard nothing for two or three weeks and, with some regret, shrugged it off, as an inner voice told me, "He's just not that into you."

First digression: Earlier on that June Friday, I'd had another reunion, engineered by my classmate Joan. My high school semi-boyfriend—flirting, prom, no other dating until his reappearance three years later—had been a skinny, acne-faced guy named Larry. Joan, who lives in Arizona, discovered that Larry and his wife did as well. Fearless and outgoing, she had tracked him down (he later confessed to me that he hadn't remembered her at first) and arranged for the two couples to get together. One afternoon Joan called me, and the next moment Larry was saying hello, sounding like the nice Jewish man from the Bronx that he was. When Larry reappeared during my college senior year, he'd made overtures about getting serious, but I was also dating two other boys, one of whom would become my husband. When Howard died I'd received a beautiful letter from Larry encouraging me to call but I never had. I hadn't thought it would thrill his wife.

A few months later, my sister and I flew to Sedona and Tucson for a few days. I couldn't pass up an opportunity to see Larry, so we met for brunch. In the intervening fifty-five years he'd held up well and, in fact, was much better looking than he had been at twenty-one.

As for the sixtieth, Larry and his wife were in New York for a family event but unable to attend the reunion. Instead, Joan and husband, and Larry and his wife and I, met for lunch at an Upper West Side deli. As we talked and laughed, not for the first time it went through my mind that, had I married Larry, I would still have a husband. Such are the strange thoughts of lonely widows.

The following February, scrolling idly on Facebook, I was stunned when a sentence jumped off my iPhone: *I said goodbye to my Uncle Larry today*, it declared. This seemingly robustly healthy soul, this man about whom I'd had momentary fantasies, had been diagnosed with a brain tumor in January and was gone in a month. It was the polar opposite of my fantasy. You really don't ever know.

As I was saying, one morning in August I found a message from Richard in my inbox. He'd been in Europe, he wrote, visiting a woman who'd been an old and dear friend of his late wife's. I was intrigued that he'd bothered telling me what his relationship was with this woman. I was beyond intrigued, actually letting out a whoop of joy, when he wrote that he'd felt the same way as I had at the reunion. He said he would be happy to join me at the opera. I sent him the roster and he selected two, for the following January and February, nearly six months ahead. I thought he might suggest that we see each other sooner, perhaps for lunch or dinner, but nothing happened. September came, and with it the Jewish holidays and another pretext. I texted a Happy New Year. He sent reciprocal greetings.

I was out of pretexts. I was not about to wish him a Happy Halloween or even Happy Thanksgiving. I was beginning to wonder if he'd forgotten about the whole thing. I put away my hopes. A few days into January, I texted to ask if he was still planning to come. He said of course, that he was in Texas visiting his sister, was returning the next night and would be in touch. About four days later he texted to ask if I'd be driving in or taking Uber, and if I planned to eat at home or to have dinner before the opera. If I wanted to eat in the city, he said, I should suggest some possible places. It was all about what my plans were, what I wanted, as though he didn't matter or care. I said I'd drive and wanted to eat in town, naming a few restaurants. He said we could firm up the arrangements as the date got closer. Two days before the opera, I gave up and texted him once again, fearing a last-minute cancellation. This was not looking promising.

The date finally arrived. While I wanted to look nice, I didn't overthink it because, clearly, he wasn't. I wore slacks and a sweater, as did he. Inevitably, because I'd allowed more than an hour to drive the ten miles to Lincoln Center, I made it in twenty minutes. I sat in my car, emailing and killing time, and finally meandered over to the restaurant, still ahead of him. When he arrived, we were seated at the end of a table that could probably accommodate thirty or forty. We joked that we must be unknowingly hosting a giant dinner party.

Because I have a hand tremor and consequent difficulties cutting food, I'm usually very careful ordering, especially if I'm not with a close friend. It was a quasi-French restaurant, and among the menu items was something called a *tartine*, which Richard, fluent in French, told me was an open sandwich. I thought I'd give it a try because the ingredients sounded tasty. *Big* mistake. The bread triangles had not been fully detached from each other. I had problems pulling or cutting them apart. Each triangle was coated with avocado, slippery food. On top of that were cucumber slices and salad greens. I tried stabbing the salad food with a fork, but most of it escaped, forming a corona around my plate. Did I say the plate was too small? Some of the food also landed in my lap, and one piece apparently made it to my neck, as Richard gently informed me. Rather than wiping it off, he kept directing me until I found it. (Was he repelled? Did he not want to touch me?)

After the greens were gone, I picked up each bread triangle and avocado, managing to get it into my mouth but leaving my hand greasy and slippery. By the time I'd finished one triangle my napkin was unusable. Richard was good enough to bring me another few napkins. With great relief, I finally finished eating the mess and the waitress came and efficiently cleaned up the table.

To my surprise, I noticed that much of Richard's conversation was medical, discussing aches and pains and an assortment of doctors. Did he have a medical problem? I also asked him about his family and learned that he was the primary babysitter, although the grandchildren wouldn't need that much longer. It was a pleasant but slightly stilted conversation, nothing like the fun we'd had at the reunion brunch.

After he paid the bill, we put on our coats to leave. As is always the case, I struggled to find my second sleeve. Usually people automatically help me, even strangers. Richard, however, didn't seem to notice a problem until I asked for his assistance, which he then gave willingly enough. OK, maybe he wasn't afraid to touch me.

As we crossed Broadway and headed for the Met, I couldn't help feeling let down, but once we made our way to our seats, the vibe changed. The stage set was visible and weird, and we bantered, coming up with silly reasons for the dozens of chairs piled all over what appeared to be a garbage dump. In the twenty minutes before the opera began I started to feel good again. It was *Wozzeck*, not the most melodious selection on the roster, but we both were curious about it. There were no intermissions but tiny breaks between acts, just long enough to mutter wisecracks to one another. Throughout most of the opera, our shoulders and upper arms touched. I was acutely aware of it, comfortable in fact, but I doubt that he noticed the contact. At the end, we agreed that we were glad we had seen *Wozzeck* and had no need to see it again—ever.

After the opera, Richard was again oblivious to the fact that I needed a little sleeve help, so I did my usual coat dance, bending over and flapping my arm until I could pull the sleeve up to my shoulder. My car was in the Lincoln Center garage, and he would be taking the subway to his home in lower Manhattan. I wondered if he'd walk me to my car, but no. (Did he not like me? Was he just a clod?) He wasn't sure how to get to the subway from underground, so I gave him directions. He thanked me, said he'd see me in two weeks, and left. A little kiss might've been nice, I thought, or a handshake, or some indication that he was looking forward to seeing me again. (Was he shy? Was he put off by my inability to eat neatly? Was there a woman in his life?) The second opera would tell me more. I was curious to see what would happen. I didn't hear from him during the two weeks.

With the *Marriage of Figaro* approaching, I sent a text suggesting that we eat at Shun Lee, an overpriced upscale Chinese restaurant near Lincoln Center. As neither one of us enjoys eating early, I said that we could just have appetizers, which appealed to him. Even I was taken aback by a six-dollar egg roll, but we had a good time at dinner. And finally, I made some inroads. Unprompted, Richard started to talk about how, when his wife first died, well-meaning friends had tried to fix him up. Unlike many men, he had no interest in meeting women. He and his wife had met as high school freshman; his relationship with her spanned over 50 years. As far as he was concerned, that part of his life was over, he said, but then added that he had briefly dated one of our other classmates. I allowed myself a sliver of hope.

I told him that I wasn't looking for a great romance, that initially I'd hoped for another relationship but really didn't care that much anymore. It was half true; I was not frantically seeking a romantic partner, but of course if one happened to fall into my lap or, more likely, I into his, I wouldn't say no. With that, he relaxed, and the warm feeling he had elicited from me at the reunion resurfaced. We agreed it would be nice to see each other, and I dared to ask him if I'd have to wait until the next opera season for that to happen. He said definitely not, and we talked about going to museums together. That was before Covid.

SECOND DIGRESSION: THERE WAS A REASON that I could say convincingly that a romantic relationship didn't matter to me. The physical part, the craving for touch, was being taken care of to a degree by an old friend, Joel. We'd had a long and close relationship, until his wife died at least, at which point it had taken all of ten months for him to notice and respond to a woman twelve years his junior who was (to my mind at least) stalking him. Joel had no further need of me. For many months I couldn't speak a word to him, but when some mutual friends started to die, we were inevitably drawn together, like a once-married couple. A year or so after my husband's death, I told Joel that I needed a hug and, girlfriend notwithstanding, he was happy to oblige. It's adolescent sex, the "everything but" variety that today probably exists only among certain religious sects, but at least—until the virus—I was getting my quota of kisses and caresses. I didn't need Richard for that.

SPEAKING OF RICHARD, AS WE LEFT the *Marriage of Figaro*, I tried again to have him walk me to my car by offering to drop him at the subway. Nothing. However, all was not lost. He smilingly said I would definitely hear from him before the next opera season. And, unless I misread it, he ever so slightly leaned towards me, perhaps for a handshake, even a little hug, but I stood frozen in my spot and he leaned back again. Two could play this game. God, it was high school all over again.

I was surprised and delighted when he texted me about

two weeks later, suggesting an exhibit at the Met (museum this time) that we might enjoy. He thought it would be fun if we met there in the morning and then had lunch together. Progress! Except. . . .

This was early March 2020, just as awareness of Covid was building. As I was pondering postponing our non-date, he texted with the same idea. Two days later, the museum closed. He decamped with his daughter upstate. I fled with my son and his family to my summer home in Connecticut. And there things remained.

It seemed pretty clear that he was not averse to hearing from me, so I did text in May to ask him how things were going. All was well, if boring. Like me, he was glad for the time with the grandkids. I responded to his response but heard nothing back, and I'd be damned if I'd text him again. So much for a budding friendship. If this plague ever truly receded, I thought, maybe we'd resume our cautious friendship. At that point, as with so many other things in those days, I had no idea what to expect down the road—if there even was a road. The Met Museum was opening soon; the Met Opera in January, they said. Maybe.

I suspect that you are looking for an end to my story. I'm looking for it myself, or perhaps a beginning. In August 2020, a year after the reunion, like so many other stories, this one had stopped in its tracks. Until that March, *carpe diem* had been my mantra, but I was afraid that *diem* would have to wait. It was frustrating; at this age, there's not a lot of time to waste.

Two years later, Richard and I had our own reunion at the Museum of Modern Art. We see each other a few times a year.

Moving to the Beat

I'M A MUSICIAN. Though neither superstar nor even mini-star, I've played one instrument or another, first piano but primarily flute and a bit of guitar, since I was eight years old. Arthritis forced me to give up playing about twenty years ago, but even now, when I hear music, I'm compelled to move.

When my dad was in a long-term care facility, my husband and I visited one day when they had a singer/guitarist performing. His music had a good beat, and I couldn't sit still. I grabbed my husband's hand and we got up and danced. My parents were smiling at us, and afterwards the recreational therapist thanked us and said that people had gotten a big kick out of watching us. I was glad to hear it, but I'd always want to be out on the floor, moving to the beat.

One of the saddest moments of my husband's last few

years was the night I pulled him and his walker onto a dance floor and after just a minute or two he, who loved to dance, begged to stop. He said, so sadly, "This is torture." His dancing days were over.

And then there was our final cruise, when we stopped to hear the band one evening. I had to get up; I danced around him as he sat on his walker. It was bitter-sweet until a stranger came over and said, "We've so enjoyed watching you, I want to give you a bottle of champagne," and he did. Bitter-sweet became sweet.

Howard's and my relationship was founded on dancing. One Fourth of July weekend, when I had gone with my aunt and uncle, and sister and her fiancé, to a dance at the Putnam Country Club in Lake Mahopac, New York, I was hanging around, bored out of my mind, when my uncle came over, shlepping this tall, gawky soldier behind him. I was just out of high school and he a year out of college, home on leave from Army basic training. I saw bottle-bottom glasses, thick lips and a significant Adam's apple. We had very little to talk about. I was a musician and he was a jock, and compounding that, we were both shy.

What saved us was dancing. I loved to dance and he moved really well, with unexpected grace and a great sense of rhythm. When the music was slow, I loved having his arms around me, his bigness making me feel safe, somehow. In fifty-two years, that never changed.

My sister had taught me to dance, and I assumed that he'd learned from his own older sister as well. Five decades later, I found out that he had secretly taken lessons at the then-famous Arthur Murray Dance Studio. He'd never told his parents. I wonder where they thought he had learned to dance?

Perhaps because we were both tall, people used to watch us, especially when we did the lindy. Not that Howard threw me over his shoulder or anything; we just moved well together. Even prior to the six knee surgeries that began in my forties, I could still dance, because you don't need to move with an even gait when you're dancing. The dance steps masked my limp.

These days when I walk, particularly if my step slows, I sing to get moving. I sing marches, folk songs, ballads, whatever sets my pace. And so it was that when my husband was recovering from major spine surgery and the physical therapists were working so hard to get him moving, I walked backwards in front of him in the hospital hallway in a parody of our dancing days, he in a hospital gown that barely reached his knees, leaning on his walker, and I softly singing my songs. He always tended to lean forward and had become quite bent over, so to get him to stand straighter I'd ask him to kiss my forehead (I was taller then) so he would stretch himself up and plant a kiss on me. The therapists thought we were adorable, but I was deadly serious. I was determined to make him walk.

On one of our forays a doctor came hurrying through the hallway. He suddenly stopped in his tracks, turned around, and asked, "Is somebody singing?" I explained.

He looked bemused and went on his way, with no apparent understanding of the power of music.

There we were, making our way down the hall with me quietly singing "Stars and Stripes Forever," the marine, army, navy and air force hymns, and a variety of other songs at different tempos. *Over hill, over dale, as we hit the dusty trail, and the caissons go rolling along*. . .as a one-time school music teacher, I had quite a repertoire. Initially, my marching songs didn't march. Rather, I stretched out notes and words like a 78 RPM record played on a turntable going 45 (figure that out, millennials!), matching his steps. We laughed at how silly it sounded as the caissons went creeping along. As he walked faster I picked up the pace, and as I did, he picked up his as well. He never became a speed walker, but he managed to keep moving until the last two months of his life.

NOW I'M ALONE, AND AS I WRITE, a new word has entered the collective vocabulary: *self-isolation*. We're in the middle of a pandemic, and everyone, particularly those of a certain age (when did I become elderly?), are cajoled, begged, ordered, to stay in their homes. On nice days, I go outside for a half-hour walk or so. I return ready for whatever awaits me.

I've noticed, three years after my husband's death, that my own pace is slower than it used to be. I have artificial knees, arthritic ankles and feet, and some lower back issues. I'm not sure which, or how many, are at the root of my slower walking. I get a little annoyed with myself when I walk along and make so little progress. I want to stride as I once did.

The second time I was out, I realized what was missing—music. My friend Marsha listens to marches when she walks. She has a collection on her phone. I have my local PBS station on my phone, so I turned it on, looking for some music, as they broadcast old standards every day. I was pleased with myself when I thought of this solution. I had my phone in my pocket and my hearing aids in my ears, the two connected by Bluetooth. No wires, no things protruding from my ears that make me look like an alien. Just barely visible hearing aids. I turned on the music, put the phone in my pocket, and off I went.

But one thing was wrong: As I listened to song after song, I couldn't walk to them. I'd never heard such tempos. Years ago, when my husband and I, both of us dancing fools, would be at an event, when the band started to play, we'd look at each other and say, "OK, what's this?" As soon as we'd established whether it was a foxtrot (boy, am I dating myself), lindy, cha-cha, or other dance, we'd be out on the floor. Now as I listened to the beginning of each song, trying to feel the beat, I couldn't do it. I heard dreamy ballads in which the singer bent the tempos, terrific jazz riffs that meandered all over the rhythmic palette, but nothing with a walking pace. Some great dance music, though, so as I walked along my sidewalk-less suburban street, I found myself stopping to do a few dance steps, walking a bit more, dancing some more, until I got self-conscious. Was someone looking out the window wondering who that weird lady was? Or was one of the young couples I know who seem to keep an eye on me (both lovely and dismaying) wondering if perhaps I'd lost it? Also, when you dance, you don't have a whole lot of forward motion, so I could only do it at intervals, with walking steps between dance steps, semi-hiding between parked cars.

Finally, today, I was walking, actually trying to ignore the music because I couldn't walk to it, and a song began—I don't even know what it was—and the baritone voice gave me my tempo. I was delighted. It carried me for about three quarters of a long block, by which time I was almost home. When the song ended, I stuck to the pace, and before I knew it I was unlocking my door, smiling and energized.

Where would we be without music? I know where I'd be. Standing still.

A Single Woman—Recapitulation

I DON'T KNOW IF I'D CALL this evolution an interesting process, but a process it certainly is. Not *has been*, but *is*, because it's still going on and may continue for the rest of my life for all I know.

Howard died two months after successful surgery for tongue cancer. But he'd been so debilitated after months of not eating due to pain in his tongue that he was malnourished and unable to recover from a host of postsurgical after-effects. I was also starting to see signs of cognitive decline, particularly in his driving. The last year or two of his life were very scary for me, as I feared I'd become a widow. I was, sadly, correct.

That label *widow* is still strange to me. I had no widow role models. My grandmother had become a widow at an early age when her husband contracted meningitis, years before I was born. It seemed a part of her identity, not something that had happened to her, as though she had been *born* a widow. My parents were married for sixty-six years and died three days apart. Even though my mother survived my father for that brief period, she didn't know of his death and obviously never had time to experience widowhood. My sister was twice divorced but never widowed. My aunt died before my uncle, and then he quickly remarried, twice.

I don't have any first cousins, but my mother had many, and when I think about it, I realize that nearly every couple suffered the loss of the wife rather than the husband, often past the age of ninety. Statistically, that's pretty remarkable. Consequently, I took it for granted that Howard and I would last a long time and then I might go first because I was the one with chronic disease.

When Howard died, I admit to feeling an element of relief along with the grief. The shoe had dropped, but I was still standing. Looking back, I realize that I was shocked, though I never would have used that word three years ago. I don't think I could comprehend this new persona; mostly, I now realize, I thought of it as a temporary state, like being in limbo.

While I never had thoughts of remarrying or even living with another man—well, maybe living—for some stupid reason I was confident that I would have a relationship again, as I've noted. Even though I'd been a classic wallflower as a young woman, as I matured, I don't think I'm deluding myself when I say that men liked me, and I liked a few of them, too. But once on my own, I didn't consider some important factors, such as most of them still being married, or the axiom that most widowers, having been stunned that they outlived their wives, only wanted somebody considerably younger than themselves for their next stage. Or that my extremely arthritic and tremulous hands made me look less than healthy and more than my age. Yes, I'm smart and funny, financially independent, and have a decent figure for this stage of life, but one could say that about a lot of other women who also have graceful and steady hands, who don't have to sit down during a hike because of aching ankles or knees, who like to cook, and who have the stamina of a race horse.

Having made a study of the situation, I've learned that there seems to be only one environment in which physical limitations don't matter, and that's in places like continuing care retirement communities or assisted living facilities. So many people there drive scooters or walk with walkers and canes that it's the norm rather than the exception. In such places, like the community in which my best friend lives, seeing two scooters snuggled overnight outside an apartment in which a couple of ninety-year-olds are inside imitating their scooters is far more likely to raise a cheer than an eyebrow. So yes, I could probably move to such a place, but so far the trade-off of living a somewhat regimented, if also positive, lifestyle in order to have a man in my life is just not worth it. Pretty funny when you think of it; move to the old folks' home to find a boyfriend. Maybe someday, but not now. Not for me dinner scheduled from five to seven, meaning you show up at five and finish by seven. Not for me *mah jongg* or canasta, and I'm not smart enough to learn bridge. I still want to take myself and a friend to concerts, theater, and the opera, no matter how convenient and easy it is to go on a bus with the rest of the old people. I guess I'm in denial, and so what.

Six months after Howard died I checked out J-Date and Match.com. The first didn't work for me at all; I never found anyone who intrigued me, nor did I seem to intrigue anyone else. Panicked as I approached the midpoint between seventy and eighty, I dared not wait any longer lest I be permanently out of the running. I carefully calculated my appearance: do they like women in skirts rather than slacks? What do I do about the fact that I can't wear heels and they're more flattering? Then again, if I'm not so tall, maybe I'm more appealing. Should I let my hair grow? Men seem to like longer hair. Do I put on enough makeup to have a more finished appearance, or would this particular guy go for a more natural look? After decades in which I had grown to be comfortable with myself, I bounced right back to the self-conscious sixteen-year-old I once was.

The dates were not so horrible as some women have said, but neither were they satisfying. The best time in online dating is that period between when you reach out to each other but before you've actually met. It's filled with possibilities. But even if you go into it with no expectations, which I quickly learned to do, disappointment, or at best boredom, is usually the outcome. I got through it because it provided fodder for my writing. That actually made it fun as I thought of colorful and sometimes vindictive ways of describing these various men. Eventually I decided to back off, but I admit that the pictures they continued to send occasionally drew me in. Obviously, meeting someone personally rather than online is a more felicitous way to date, but to say it narrows your options is a vast understatement.

Meanwhile, I had surgery to remove a rheumatoid nodule, or growth, in an embarrassing place, and then to replace a knee, which is at least commonplace. I grew a few wrinkles. I literally slowed down, as my pace became shorter and my steps slower. Without Howard to mask my arthritic challenges when putting on socks and boots, or help me into or out of more form fitting clothing, my wardrobe got looser and my shoes clunkier. Two fingers on my right hand lost the ability to type and made cutting food and eating it even more awkward. As each of these new limitations developed, I'd get depressed, get used to it, and be okay until the next time I lost some ability. And then I had an epiphany: With each loss, my first thought was that now I would be even more unappealing to a man. It was all about the men. Suddenly, I realized that, if I took the man out of the equation, the wrinkles and messed-up hands shrank, in significance if not in actuality. It was astonishingly liberating.

Armed with my new perspective, I looked again at my

situation. All around me, all over the world in fact, are single people. Some of them have never married and may never do so. Some have divorced. And lots and lots, among them several wonderfully supportive women friends, have been widowed and are in various stages of learning to live without the other half of their relationship. Some will find romance, but the majority, especially the women, will not. The trick, I've learned, is to build a beautiful life that doesn't require an opposite image, a life that is full and joyous *on its own.* And that's what I've decided to do. I'm sick of trying to define the word *widow*; I'm finished doing that. Widowhood implies bereavement; singlehood might be lonely, but there is no automatic implication of grief.

Widows are often at a later point on life's continuum; singles can be twenty-one. In my own mind at least, and according to my therapist, many widows are fearful of trying new things, of dating, dining, or going to a movie alone, of traveling. I admit that I haven't attempted to travel solo. I don't know if being alone in an unfamiliar place unnerves me, or if it's because of my need for assistance with luggage and sometimes a wheelchair when navigating larger airports. But I'm looking into possibilities. Rarely do I dine out alone, but I suspect I will eventually.

I would do these things even if I called myself a widow, but I just don't feel like it's an accurate description anymore. I miss Howard; in some ways I miss him more than I did a year or two ago, but it's been a long time since I sat on the couch in my den, crying and shrieking to him, "How could you have *abandoned* me this way!"

I'm throwing away that label. I feel like I'm emerging from a forest of obstacles into a meadow of possibilities. I am, simply, a strong, competent, funny, fairly attractive single woman. So here's to me, and to you as well.

So Then What Happened?—December, 2023

PERHAPS YOU, LIKE ME, SOMETIMES ARRIVE at the end of a book longing to know what happens next. How do the characters go on with their lives? Do they live happily ever after, descend into the abyss, or just continue on their way? I'm not where I was when I wrote these essays, so I felt compelled to provide a taste of the next leg of the journey.

Probably most important is that it appears I've become a writer. I can no longer play music or sing, but that loss led me in a new, deeply rewarding direction—a classic example of the cliché about open and closed doors and windows.

Here I am, seven years out and seven years older, reading this once again before publication. With the passage of time I travel farther and farther from where I left

Howard, as though he's back at the station, having missed the train. There's so much I want to tell him. In fact, I *do* tell him, usually at the cemetery, how much I miss him and often wish I could have a do-over in which I take better care of him. I speak of our grandson Franklin, now living and working in Chicago, who has inherited his sweet nature as well as his considerable height; or his sister Nora, an artist like her brother and their parents; about sometimes surprising turns of events, including the writing; even gossip about our friends, laughing at myself while I do so. (At least I don't expect an answer.) And when I say good-bye I actually kiss the cold tombstone. Never would I have thought. . .I'm an old lady who kisses tombstones!

Anyone who has lost someone special will agree that celebrating milestones always produces a pang. Howard was seventy-nine when he died, and we had thought he would turn eighty, I seventy-five, and Edward fifty, all in the same year. What a big party we'd have had.

He'd have loved the fact that our youngest grandchild, Maya, whom he named "Mayapapaya," treasures that name and gives me the exclusive grandparental privilege of using it.

In eulogizing Howard, I wrote that I married my greatest fan. He'd have gotten a kick out the writing, I think, which really started on the heels of his death. (I still say "death," by the way; Howard did not "pass" to any other life that I know of. He died, as everything animate does.) Had he remained alive, I might never have explored my feelings by writing essays. For me, writing relieved the pressure bearing down on me in the first months of loss.

I never would have taken some of the new directions or gotten to know some of the new people who comprise my life now. That would've been a different kind of loss, even though I'd never have known it. I wish so that we could have endured Covid together, as it was such a lonely time, though given his frailty, he may not have survived. I'm glad he was not a Covid statistic.

I've had a few health challenges of my own, including three bouts of Covid, one case of shingles, and an orthopedic surprise in the form of suddenly needing a new hip to add to my artificial joint collection. I wonder if any of that was an outgrowth of grief-induced stress. Yet the anger—at fate, utility companies, insurance providers, even at Howard—that had a habit of bubbling up in the first few years has diminished if not dissipated.

I've remained in my one-level home, which I love, but acknowledge the possibility of some day moving to an independent living community. I look at friends who are older than I am, still living in their two-story houses, and say to myself that if they can do it, so can I. The reality is, however, that I have physical limitations. I thought that, by this stage of life, the playing field would level, but it hasn't. As my cohort and I all say to each other, "Everybody has something," but if you can still climb stairs and get up from chairs, reach upper shelves, bend to pick things up, and open jars and childproof medicine containers (maybe that most of all), you don't have to leave your home of many years. At least not yet. As for me, I'm on the cusp.

Whether because of age or circumstance, I don't have the craving for a special someone in my life the way I did for the first five years or so. In addition to my friend Richard, along the way I developed a friendship with a man name Steve. It was looking promising in the relationship department but, sadly, I recently received news that Steve died. I had not heard from him in two weeks, which was atypical. Eventually I started checking the obits, as one does at this stage. His turned up after about a week. Not knowing any of his family or friends, I don't know the exact circumstances. It's a sad loss. Maybe having had these two friends, plus another man who comes over here and embraces me now and then, met the need for intellectual and physical stimulation. If a romantic partner miraculously turned up in my life, I certainly wouldn't fight it, but it's much more of a want than a need now.

My sister, older by several years but always the stronger and healthier one, was killed by cancer three years ago. I miss her enormously because we had so much fun laughing together and could tell each other our secrets, yet, for the first time since I was born, I'm not in her shadow. And I don't have to deal with people mistakenly asking me how much older I am than she is. I'm finding out who I am without having to factor in my dynamic sibling. I admit that I'm grateful to have had this opportunity to know myself better.

There's been a lot of death, of course. That's life. Sometimes I feel stalked by it. I've been worried about taking too long to publish this book because I don't want it to be posthumous. I try hard to act as though I have a future, but when you pass eighty, especially if you have a less than glowing health history, it's hard to maintain that mindset.

Then again, I have a friend who had his first heart attack in his fifties and has also recovered from stomach cancer. He's now a few years past ninety, bopping along on his walker, so you never know. I see the changes in my face, the dryness of my skin, and note the assistance that I sometimes need with stairs, chairs, jars, and coat sleeves, and I wonder. And then I see another ninety-plus friend who is in a wheelchair and has a full-time aide, who's as delightful as ever, and I stop worrying about my skin.

I'm again shopping for a new car. I acquired a jazzy red Prius that I still get a kick out of, loving the self-image it provides, but I must confess it's not the car for me. It's too low; it doesn't have power seats or a power trunk, which for me are necessities, not luxuries. It's back to SUV-land for me, and I regret the need. My son has come with me to look at cars. I don't have to prove that I can get one on my own, and I'm grateful for his know-how, to say nothing of his company, but I also noticed that two of the car salesmen addressed the conversation to him until I reminded them that the car is for me. So what else is new?

I was going to write that things bother me less than they used to, from doctors who don't call back to friends who disappoint, but I think what's actually happening is that, whenever possible, I avoid people and situations that upset me. I just don't have time for them. I think I've become more mellow, though I don't know if my friends would agree.

I've also become somewhat reclusive since Covid. I'm not afraid to go out, but for reasons I can't explain, I look for excuses to stay home. Maybe that'll be the subject of my next piece. Everything, as I've said, is fodder.

I still prefer people to animals, but I've noticed that I now comment if I see a cute dog or a beautiful cat, a new behavior. I shake my head in wonder when I hear myself discussing my cavapoo grand-dog Clayton's toy-like face or ability to levitate when he gets excited. I even showed a friend a picture of him recently! Something similar happened when I was in my fifties. All of a sudden, a grandmother hormone kicked in, and I started cooing over babies in stores and restaurants. My friend Stef, who has always adored babies in addition to animals, almost fainted. Prior to that, the only babies who'd provoked cooing in me were my own.

I'm still writing essays, but I had to stop somewhere if I wanted to publish, so here it is. I hope you've enjoyed reading them. For those in mourning, I hope they've brought a laugh now and then. I was once asked to read the piece about a thousand napkins to my bereavement group. Among the dozen or so people in the room was a relatively young woman whose loss was fresh. Her default facial expression was no expression at all. She didn't seem tuned in to the conversation. While hearing about the napkins that refused to get used up, she started to laugh. It was the first time I had seen her smile. Another woman in the group, about twenty-five years my junior, came to me after another reading and said, "You're writing about my life!" Wow. I can have an impact. That's why I decided to publish.

Widowhood, this altered state of being, can be sad and isolating, but if we allow ourselves to acknowledge the humor in the absurdities of life now, it can bring new adventures here and there, even from our armchairs. Keep an eye out for them.

And I even took a trip to Iceland. But that's another story.

www.ingramcontent.com/pod-product-compliance
Lightning Source LLC
LaVergne TN
LVHW091323150826
845673LV00006B/1748

* 9 7 9 8 2 1 8 4 7 2 5 0 4 *